The Lost Cause Chronicles:

Confessions of the Problem Child

Lauren Lajas

Disclaimer

Introduction

A hill that I will die on is that children are and remain blameless. As I tell my story, I admit the exact moment where I felt I started to be responsible for my own actions. I had to grow up super quickly and decide at an early age who I wanted to be. Was I going to be a broken child for the rest of my life? Would I refuse to heal from my wounds and let them fester, bleeding on everyone I came in contact with? I spent a good part of my childhood doing just that. Lashing out. Getting into fights. Being closed off. No one could tell me anything. But let me reiterate, I will always consider myself blameless during this period of my life. I was the victim. I was born with ferocious demons. Demons that still torment me to this very day. I had to go through things that even grown adults wouldn't have survived. I had to process emotions I wasn't even aware of yet. The kicker is that children become adults if they're lucky. I was taught right from wrong. I would feel my conscience. I would learn how to cope. I was robbed of many choices. A happy childhood. Parents who loved me. A stable upbringing. Cheerful holidays and family vacations. But a time came when I could choose to remain a victim of my circumstances and be defined by my past. Don't get me wrong, I am most definitely a product of my environment, and my past most certainly defines me. But I chose to let it influence me for the better. I was told once that a lot of people can overcome obstacles, but it takes a certain strength to be able to talk about it after the fact. To share your story. Not everyone has THAT type of strength. For a very long time, I was angry at God and the universe. They are interchangeable to me so whatever your belief system, go with me on this. Why was I the one they chose to have the childhood and adolescence that I had? Couldn't they have chosen someone else? Be careful what questions you ask if you aren't prepared for the answers. I was angry until i understood my purpose. I already knew the answer but from time to time, i need to be reminded of it. I was listening to a sermon once, and the pastor was talking about how some of us have had harder lives and thougher battles because God knew we could not only persevere but be strong enough to show others how they too can overcome their obstacles. Forged under such darkness, I was meant to be a beacon of hope. To shine so brightly so others could see that there is indeed a light at the end of the tunnel. An end to their suffering. A way to come out even stronger and more powerful than before.

Let's get a few things out of the way. I want to start off by saying that I am in no way, shape, or form, attacking anyone's character. That is not my intention. I am simply telling MY story the way I saw it, felt it, and lived through it. My conscience is now clear to say what I have to say freely because two out of the three women I am going to discuss in length have passed away. I never met the third one, so forgive me if I never considered her feelings. I am blunt, assertive, and say what I need to say. It is a gift and a curse. But I am not reckless with my words. I have thought about them for years. Decades even. I truly believe there was a purpose to my pain, and the first step was to share it in the manner i felt most comfortable with. I cried (a lot). I have been so consumed by anger that i even started to scare myself. I hid away when i felt too numb for any form of human interaction. I drank (a lot). But I have come up on the other side, and such a weight has been lifted from my shoulders. I pride myself on being considered as one of the strong ones. Especially with all I have been through. People often commend me for my resilience and mental toughness but the truth is, I wasn't really given a choice to be any other way. One of my coping mechanisms is through humor. I am light-hearted for the most part, so I, in turn, make light of most situations. Even the ones I shouldn't. The reason I bring this up is that I will not apologize for cracking a joke or sounding a bit harsh in certain moments while talking about very serious issues. It's who I am; love me or leave me. Most importantly, I want to state that I was a child. An innocent life dealt an arduous hand from birth. I did the best I could while having to deal with circumstances a child never should have to deal with. But I did. I am a survivor. I hate describing myself as such, if I'm going to be honest because that term implies I was a victim at some point. And if I struggle with painting myself as a survivor, in my mind, a victim is far worse. But that is what I am. A victim. And this is my story (*cue Law and Order SVU theme music*). I am going to state the obvious: I have severe mommy issues. Mommy issues on steroids. Mommy issues on crack, which is fitting because I just so happen to be a crack baby (I have been making crack baby jokes my whole life, so don't start judging me now). But hey, they are what make me, me! I owe my resilient nature and mental toughness to them. I have a knack for finding humor and light in almost any situation, like being a crack baby... ok ok, I'm done. But nevertheless, I have had to do a lot of inner work to be a functioning member of society. It hasn't been easy. And a lot of times, it wasn't pretty. Being treated in such a way by a woman who was supposed to love, guide, and protect you alters the very foundation of who you are as a person, as a woman. And I had that happen to me not once, not twice, but three times. A woman usually doesn't wake up and go, "Hey, I'm going to physically and mentally abuse my kids today." At least not a sane one. But it happens. More often than you think. A moment of complete honesty here, but it is one of the reasons I am hesitant about being a mother myself. You can truly be a good person and have the purest of intentions, yet something goes wrong, and the children are the ones who suffer for it. The cycle of domestic violence is a cycle for a reason. While I personally feel strong and self-aware enough to be the one who breaks that cycle, why risk it? Not every person who had a similar upbringing like I did makes it out alive. Makes it out to be able to live a normal life. Despite everything, I consider myself one of the lucky ones. I wouldn't be standing here today without these women. Literally and figuratively. As I go through each "mother's" chapter, I will end it on a positive note, so bear with me. I owe everything I am and everything I have yet to become to them. It has taken a lot of personal growth to be able to admit that, but it is true. It is absolutely and unequivocally true.

Another moment of sheer honesty and vulnerability...It took me way longer than I thought to get my story onto paper. Not just because it was hard for me to sit with these memories for long periods of time; that is obvious. But it was because I went back and forth on if I wanted to tell it in the first place. Telling a non-fictional story means you have to tell it all, the good, the bad, the ugly. The parts that may paint you in a certain light. The parts that remain hidden from the world. The parts that only make an appearance in the middle of the night when I can't sleep. The parts I have never said out loud.

I am a very proud person. Pride is my most toxic trait and my most fatal flaw. I am a very private person as well. Not too many people know the full extent of my story, not even those closest to me. I carry myself in such a way that you would never know I have the backstory that I have. I have been told that by almost everyone I let in, and I love that for me. It is a reminder to myself that I, indeed, came up on the other side, a strong and beautiful woman. Society has painted people who grew up "in the system" in a certain light, whether that was intentional or not. I have personally witnessed people's eyes change when I mention I grew up in foster care or was adopted. Most of the time, it's pity, but I have also encountered fear. Or maybe alarm if that makes sense. Either way, I hated it. I also just mentioned how I hate branding myself as a victim or a survivor, but in truth, it's because I then will have to admit that I had something to survive. I allowed things to happen to me that made me a victim. One of the things that gets talked about very little is how a lot of victims blame themselves. What could I have done differently? Maybe it was my fault. How could I have allowed these things to happen to me? And the one thought that will always loom in the back of my mind, "why wasn't I good enough?"

Even saying that out loud is a direct hit to my pride. If I'm truly as strong and mentally tough as I like to think I am, how can I display this type of weakness? A true lady never reveals her secrets, and here I am, about to divulge them all. Part of this healing journey was to learn how to forgive those I felt didn't deserve my forgiveness, to accept apologies I would never hear, and to redefine what closure meant to me because the closure I thought I needed, I would never receive. But the most important part was to learn how to forgive that fiery little girl. To forgive myself. And that was when the true healing began.

THE BIRTH MOTHER

Chapter 1

I never met my biological mother. I don't know anything about her except her name. Maria, which could have been an alias or a name she gave the hospital. I tried to look her up once, and the results were laughable. I am from a small town in the middle of nowhere in Florida, so I was hopeful…4000 hits in my county alone. Basically, "Maria (last name omitted for obvious reasons" is the Hispanic version of "Jane Doe." What I know of her was that she was a drug addict and a prostitute. Having been born with multiple venereal diseases and crack-cocaine in my system, I knew this to be true. I also had it confirmed when I went to college. I was a first-generation student and had to prove I was a ward of the state to apply for extra scholarships. So here I was, a 17-year-old kid, on my way to the clerk of courts to ask for my foster care documents. What I found broke my heart. For the first time, in black and white, I read the humble beginnings of my parentage. My birthname was actually Lorraine. Thank goodness that got changed.

I indeed was born with syphilis, gonorrhea, and chlamydia. An HIV test was also run, which came back negative. I guess that's the silver lining. Both my sister and I were born with crack-cocaine in our systems. We were crack babies. For some reason I was given a few of her documents as well, but I won't go into any detail regarding her. That's her own story to tell in her own time. Father unknown. That of course, was expected. What came after that was what had me in a catatonic-like state for days. My birth mom gave up her parental rights upon my birth (again, no shocker there), and I was immediately placed into foster care. She was given two chances to go to court and prove that she might have cleaned up her act to possibly be an adequate mother so she could get her newborn daughter back, and she didn't bother to show up to either one.

I have seen my baby pictures. I was adorable. Obviously, I am biased, but I was a cute, blameless, innocent baby. I don't know if she even bothered to hold me. I am not familiar with these types of proceedings. Was she allowed to say goodbye? Did she even want to? Was there any moment that she fought to keep me, even in her condition? Do you sign over your parental rights before or after you've had a chance to see your own flesh and blood? I was beside myself. How could a mother give up on her newborn child? How could a grown adult allow themselves to get so low in life to resort to drug use of that caliber? How could she still violate her body and let countless men use and abuse her in that way, knowing that she was pregnant? Did my little life mean nothing? They talk about the instant bond a mother feels at that moment. An automatic connection with someone you know you will love for a lifetime. A maternal instinct supposedly kicks in. So...what happened here? Why was I not good enough? What was so wrong with me that she didn't get the new mommy memo? I had to stay in the hospital a little longer to detox as well as be treated for venereal diseases. Once I got a clean bill of health, I was sent on my way to start my foster care journey.

Chapter 2

I don't remember too much about this part of my childhood. How could I? I was an infant that was immediately put into the system. The Foster Care system. I was put in multiple foster homes before I was adopted. As a foster parent, you're given a stipend, usually monthly, for expenses that will occur when caring for a child. Because of my condition, and by condition, I mean being a crack baby, I was considered "high risk," which meant the stipend would be more. Now, I am not saying this influenced people's decisions either way; I am just stating facts. While I truly believe that most people go into fostering children with the purest intentions, horror stories exist for a reason. I was placed in more homes than usual due to physical and sexual abuse. Physical abuse is easier to detect in an infant, but the process of proving sexual abuse is trickier. But having had medical exams that found more excessive trauma and irritation to my genital areas that wouldn't have otherwise been caused by your typical diaper changes and wiping proved this. I remember faces. Certain memories. I have flashbacks of some terrible occurrences that tend to haunt me at times. One of a shadowy figure looming over my crib, hurting me. I remember crying and crying and crying with no one even bothering to come check up on me or console me, a helpless baby. I have this one memory where I was covered in my own blood.

My white or light pink sheets and the nearest wall where my bed was also smeared in the same crimson substance that coated my little body. I also remember getting beaten some more because of the "mess" I had made. I would later encounter the face that was doing the beating in my red memory later in life, and I asked her about it as an adult. How it was explained to me was that it was a simple act of reprimand. I misbehaved and needed to be disciplined. The offense was that me and my sister, who were in the same foster home at the time were playing a game in which one of us was the wife and the other the husband. We just so happened to share a kiss when our foster mother walked in. Of course, we were both beaten for it because the bible says girls don't kiss other girls. We were sent to bed early, and I wouldn't stop crying, so I was given a reason to cry, which somehow led to me bleeding enough to have my nightshirt drenched along with blood all over my sheets and walls. Since I was adopted by the age of four and a half, I couldn't have been any older than three, and my little sister was two years of age. I do have happy memories. One of me is playing by myself on a playground. Running around and falling down, but giggling as I got back up, still clenching this random leaf that, in my mind, was the greatest. thing. ever. Another one where I was twirling around in a pretty dress. Falling down again and laughing about it. I have always been clumsy.

I only remember one foster family: Ruthie and Ramon. They were the foster parents I had right before I was adopted. When my sister, Nani, was born, since we were so close in age, we were bound together by the courts so we could stay together. I remember their faces and pretty dresses. Ruthie and Ramon were the God-fearing type so I'm assuming they had me in my Sunday- best all the time. This was the first time I remembered having a playmate: My sister. I do have lots of happy memories here with us playing and laughing. But my red memory also occurred here. And Ruthie was the one doing the beating. From my understanding, Ruthie and Ramon wanted to adopt me and my sister, but there was a major conflict of interest: she was also our caseworker. I am not going to pretend I know the rules and regulations or the limitations on how just involved caseworkers can get with their "cases," but one can only imagine how this could complicate an adoption.

What little I know of my biological mother, I learned from Ruthie. She was a Mexican immigrant who struggled with drug addiction. Ruthie allegedly knew the name of my biological father as well. All I was told of him was that he was a big Black man standing at 6'5 and weighing about 350 lbs. It was a running joke between the two of us for me not to date a Mexican or Black guy in my hometown because I didn't know if I'd be related to them or not. I thought of looking him up, but what would I actually say to him? "Good morning sir; remember that Hispanic woman you slept with back in 1989? Well, surprise! I'm your daughter!" There is no scenario in which I would receive the homecoming I imagined. In truth, I have no desire to meet my biological parents. What is done is done. My birth mom slept with men for drugs and money to buy drugs, and I just so happened to be a by-product of one of those transactions. Case and point. Supposedly, I have an older sister. I am the second-oldest; then comes my sister Nani, and after that comes a slew of brothers, all of us having different dads, of course. Honestly, who knows at this point? The story is she got herself clean after Nani and kept the boys but I can't confirm that. It was what Ruthie told me. I would have loved to be an older sister to my brothers, though. I would have loved the opportunity to watch sports and throw back some brewskis with the boys. Intimidate their girlfriends but beat them up if they were anything but gentlemanly behind their backs. I don't know how I'd react to having a big sister. I'd hope we'd get a long and be the best of friends. But I'm used to being the Beyonce of the group. The leader. The bossy one. You know, typical big sister behavior. The only sibling I know in person is Nani and I was robbed of the opportunity to be a big sister to her. But that chapter is coming a little bit later.

Chapter 3

What keeps me up at night sometimes regarding my birth mom is the circumstances as to how I was conceived. There was no love. No planning. No baby shower to celebrate what is normally a very joyous occasion. No picking out the wall color and décor for my nursery. Nothing. A lot of times, babies aren't always planned, but the lives of the mother and father are forever changed and then comes the altering of their lives to accommodate a usually welcomed addition to the family. I am pretty positive my biological father doesn't even know I exist, and my biological mother gave me up upon birth because she fell pregnant by a man she had sex with for money or drugs.

There was no prenatal care, seeing as how she couldn't even manage to stop her drug use during her pregnancy. I know I make crack baby jokes, but my circumstances could have been far worse. A lot of crack babies have developmental issues inside and outside of the womb and can suffer long-term health problems. They can suffer cognitive issues and learning disabilities. A lot of them die. I was born prematurely and with a very low birth weight, but by the grace of God and modern medicine, that was about it. I was born partially deaf in my left ear, but that could have been caused by anything. We have all heard stories about the drug-detox process for adults. It's riddled with pain, physically, mentally, and emotionally. Now, imagine that process being perpetrated on a newborn baby. Then there is having been born with multiple sexually transmitted diseases, which absolutely breaks my heart just thinking about that. As an adult, I take my sexual health very seriously and make sure I implement safe sex practices and keep up with my check-ups and screenings. I am a huge advocate for condoms and other forms of birth control. I am proud to say I have never had an STD since I started having sex. The health risks involved with being born with venereal diseases can be severe as well. Syphilis can cause blindless in babies that go through the birth canal if it gets in their eyes, and if left untreated, a lot of them die. They can cause brain damage. STDs such as HIV, genital herpes, and genital warts can get passed from mother to child, and they will be stuck with those diseases for the rest of their lives. There is a very harsh social stigma attached to STDs even though they are super common, so imagine having to explain to your future partners that you have genital herpes because you were born with it. But again, I am one of the lucky ones, as a simple course of antibiotics and a very brief stint in baby rehab made me as good as new! I laugh to prevent the tears, ok?

I don't know how quite to explain this, but I sometimes feel like I am in a constant identity crisis. I never feel like I belong. In any group of people or places I've been or moved to, I still just feel like I don't belong. But hey, don't feel sorry for me. I've never felt the pressure to fit in or have given myself anxiety to go with the "status-quo" because I genuinely don't care to. I know I couldn't even if I tried, and that has been absolutely freeing. Call me a free spirit: Wild of hair. Wild of heart. Or, because since birth, I was robbed of truly knowing who I was. Not a day goes by that I don't stare into the mirror and wonder if I have my mother's smile or my father's eyes. Where did my love of music and singing come from? Who's laugh do I have? From which side did I inherit my temper? Thanks a lot for that one! Or even when I go to the doctor's office, and you answer the questions about your family history, I just write, "I wouldn't know; I'm adopted." As far as what I mark on the same applications for my race and ethnicity, I've been told that my biological mother is Mexican, and my biological father is Black. Given the texture of my hair and body type, I can see the "black" genes. I have played guess-my-ethnicity with people my entire life, but I couldn't tell you honestly. I have been wanting to do a blood test on 23 and Me for years, but I chicken out because of the waivers you must sign. I have watched enough Black Mirror episodes, and I'm still not over when they tried to frame Captain Olivia Benson! But in truth, I'm afraid that I'm not what I've been told I was my entire life.

Saying I'm half black is such a broad term. I could be Jamaican, Haitian, or Sudanese, for all I know! Mexico is a vast country. It would be nice to know what part I'm from. Given my ego, I could be Aztec Royalty and not even know it! For as much appreciation as I have for different cultures, It would be nice to know my own. I just can't bring myself to deal with the potential lie I would have been told. I know I will do it one day.

I'm also afraid of the potential relatives I could meet. I have dreamed of having a family. Cousins. Aunts. Uncles. There is a saying that states not to meet your heroes. What if I meet them and they are horrible people? What if we have nothing in common? What if they just don't like me? Here we go with the cycle of abandonment all over again.

Chapter 4

Moment of truth...

I used to hold such animosity towards my birth mom. I used to hate her because of the choices she made. Her drug use. Her lifestyle. Her not even showing up at the hearings to get me back. For not having the strength or not caring enough to get her act together for the sake of her family. I blamed her for the pain and misery I would go on to endure throughout the next chapters of my life. The circumstances as to how I was made and brought into this world haunt me, and I don't think I will ever be able to get over it. I have felt shame and embarrassment my entire life when talking about how and when I was born. About never meeting my birth parents. People give you this look of disbelief. As if they couldn't possibly fathom how one doesn't know their parents if they aren't dead. Then, if I feel comfortable, I share a few of the details, and the look of disbelief turns to pity which I have hated even more. I detest the fact that I will most likely never meet or know my blood relatives. That choice was stripped away from me. To never be in a room filled with people who share the same noses or have the same obnoxious laugh. There is no greater bond than blood. Or at least that's what they say. How would I know?

The privilege of getting older is that you get wiser. Well, you're supposed to anyway. You grow out of the naiveté that youth grants you, and you learn how the world truly works. Not everything is as black and white as we're taught by adults who try to shield us from the harshness of reality. Like poverty. And addiction. I have accepted the fact that my birth mom did the best she could with the cards she was dealt. It isn't fair of me to judge when I don't know the actual extent of drug addiction and the hold it has on someone. Drug addiction touches every family, rich or poor. I have lived in a few major metropolitan cities and visited twice as many. In these types of areas, you always have an influx of homeless people, many of who are facing numerous challenges, including addiction as well. It breaks my heart to see them struggle. If my heart breaks for complete strangers, why couldn't I extend the same compassion to her? When I was in college, I worked at a little pizza place, one of my favorite jobs, with some of the greatest people I think of often. One summer, we noticed a woman who conducted "business" right outside our patio. She would get dropped off by a man and then have other people come up to her from time to time. Sometimes, she got in cars and drove off. She seemed harmless, so we let her be. Police patrolled that area often since it was off a very busy intersection anyway. Months had passed and one day, we noticed that she was pregnant. As one could imagine, I was triggered beyond belief. I began to take a particular interest and even found myself looking for her on my shifts. A few times, we had even set out slices of pizza for her. I willed her to make better life decisions. To quit working the corner and selling drugs because one day soon, her life would no longer be her own, and she would have an innocent child who would depend on her. If one child could be saved from what I went through, I wanted more than anything for it to be this one. But I watched her, day in and day out, her belly getting bigger, show up and continue to "work." I pitied her. I felt such grief and sadness for her. I realized that maybe her circumstances weren't self-imposed.

No woman in her right mind or of her own free will would choose to stand on her feet all day, 7-9 months pregnant, rain or shine, dealing with God-knows-who, for what I'm sure is very little profit. When she got really big, her male "friend" would stop by and let her sit in the back seat from time to time. Then one day, we never saw her again.

I forgive my birth mom. Despite everything, I turned out ok. She did give me life after all. I have learned the ways of the world. I now understand the hold drug addiction can have on someone. I understand the hunger in one's belly or the need for a simple roof over one's head can lead you to do some pretty desperate acts. I have practically been on my own since I was 18. I know that struggle all too well. I understand that coming to a new country may not have been the easiest. Who knows what support system she had when she got here? The "system" most definitely failed me, and it fails countless children in America. But what I came to realize as I got older is that it failed her too, and I no longer place the blame on her. She was a victim of her own circumstances, just as I was. I don't know what my life would have looked like had she chosen to keep me. I try not to dwell on such things because

I am learning not to cause myself grief over what I can't change or control. I can just simply accept it for what it is and move on. It doesn't make me any less of a person. I am a firm believer that everything happens for a reason, and it brought me to this point in my life to uplift and inspire others. I guess it's easier to accept that when you have made it to the other side. I may never get a clear picture of who I am through her eyes, but she can be proud of the woman that I have become. Perhaps she'll know who I am one day and can smile knowing I turned out to be a beautiful, caring, passionate woman who has her smile or spirit. The beauty of not meeting someone in real life is that I get to make up the picture for myself. In my mind, she was caring and kind. She knew I deserved a chance at a better life than what she could give me. She gave me up out of love although it was the hardest decision she ever made. She loved me enough to let me go. That's how I choose to remember her.

THE ADOPTIVE MOTHER

Chapter 5

I was adopted around the age of 5, but in foster care years, I might as well have been 15. See, the older you get, the least likely you are to get adopted because you have "history." The rumor is my adoptive parents only wanted my younger sister, but we were a 2-for-1 package deal, remember? I have never been able to make out the intentions of my adoptive parents, but I go based on actions, and their actions spoke to them, never really wanting me. Now, full disclosure, I was a typical foster care kid with typical foster care kid behavior. My adoptive mother told me that by this time, I was diagnosed with ADHD (Attention-Deficit Hyperactivity Disorder) and RAD (Reactive Attachment Disorder). ADHD is common, and everyone seems to know of that one. This is my personal opinion, but we have a really bad habit in this society of overly medicating our children just because they are acting like...children. I say that coming from the overly medicated, not as a parent, of course. Still, I have observed children my entire life, constantly making the comparisons of my own childhood, and were my behavioral issues really all that different? I was full of energy, to be sure. Truth be told, I still have an issue with authority, but I have learned to pick and choose my battles on that front to be a functioning member of society and keep me out of jail. We can check the defiant box. Ok, so I was hyper and defiant...seems like typical child-like behavior to me. Now add Reactive Attachment Disorder to the mix. RAD is a condition in which a child doesn't form healthy emotional relationships due to possible emotional neglect and/or abuse...of course, I struggled with forming attachments.

Look at what my life had been like already? Moving from home to home, already plagued by memories of abuse. It is often talked about how important it is for a newborn baby to be held, most times by its mother, but nurses will hold babies as well, so from the get-go, a baby feels safe. They can learn to form attachments in a healthy way. Clearly another memo that was lost on me, but I digress. So many caretakers already let me down, and I remember how closed off I was. I can still be like that, but I have come a long way from this point because, remember, I was still only 4-5 years old at this point.

The first memory I have of Dee, my adoptive mother, was at a McDonalds. I guess that was one of the last meet-and-greets before it became official. I don't remember meeting her before that point, and I don't have an early memory of my adoptive father or siblings. But I would start my journey with my new family in Miami, Fl. I remember what our house looked like there, but we didn't stay in Florida too long. The perks of the Lajas gang was that they belonged to a big family. I finally had aunts, uncles, and cousins, many who either lived in Miami or Orlando, a short distance away. I had the sweetest grandparents. It was a dream come true. I had God parents as well. My God mother was one of Dee's sisters. She was pretty and loquacious, always laughing. Always smiling. She did have such a pretty smile. My God father was her only brother, the black sheep of the family. The troublemaker. The rebel. Or so I was told. I can see why I was paired with these two, having similar personality traits of both. I took a liking to them instantly and remember them fondly. I had a whole bunch of cousins in Orlando and have fond memories with them too. A

Disney trip we all took together, at least 10 of us. Sleepovers with the female cousins, even though we were just passing through most times. I just knew we were all going to be close, making so many memories. They never made me feel like an outsider. They welcomed me from the beginning, and it felt nice to have a family. To feel loved. To not be so alone. My favorite memories were the very few holidays we all spent together. The joy and the laughter. All the photos we took. Dee had a passion for photography, so we were always taking pictures of matching sets with our hair done. You know, typically family stuff. Looking at these photos, we looked like a perfect, happy family. But we all know pictures lie, often concealing the real story.

Shortly after my sister and I were adopted, we ended up moving to Tennessee with the family. I also remember this house that we lived in at the end of a cul-de-sac on a decent portion of land. It was a two-story house with a second den area that was basically the kid's hangout. We had a trampoline in the backyard and our own rooms. Life was good. Dee was great at all things pertaining to art. She had painted my room with pink, purple, and blue hearts with a matching bed set and plenty of cute pillows. At this age, my sister was the outgoing and witty one, making friends and gelling better with my two new older brothers.

I can't really say I became close to my two brothers. They were as different as day and night. I didn't become a daddy's girl like my sister did. I remained at the edge of things, just along for the ride, not knowing my place and remaining reserved. Who knew how long this newfound happiness was going to last? Being 6 or 7 years of age at this time, I can't tell you how I already knew I was trying to play a part. Children are super perceptive and intelligent; they just don't know the adult wording for what they are feeling or seeing. Maybe I was already old enough to have understood that this wasn't my real family but not old enough to realize that sometimes blood isn't always what keeps people together. Or maybe I was just waiting for the other shoe to drop, subconsciously not wanting to get attached to this home in the event it wasn't permanent. Blame it on my age, my reactive attachment disorder, or that I just never truly felt at home or at ease with them; either way, I never really formed an attachment to the Lajas's. I did have some happy memories during my very short stay with this family. Big lavish birthday parties and holidays, except for the time I was told Santa wasn't real. That for sure ruined my Christmas. I remember my eldest brother trying to teach me how to ride a dirt bike, but of course, I floored it instead of using the brakes and ended up burning the inside of my little legs and crashing into some bushes. It was awesome! We all got on the trampoline and took turns sending each other sky-high and getting in trouble for it. The house was full of kids all the time.

Pool days during the warmer months. I always loved the water. The Lajas's were all musicians. Music was a big part of our lives. We attended a mega-church where I remember my adoptive father playing the congas. My brothers both played instruments very well and went on to keep music in their lives even till this day. This was the one area where I held my own. Dee had myself and my sister in all the church plays and kid's choirs. She pushed me to try out for the solos, and I would get them. I didn't know at the time just how important music would become to me, that it would be my literal lifeline. I had dreams of us starting a band as a family, with me being the front woman, writing songs together and traveling the world, performing our music. That would obviously never happen but it's a fantasy I hold onto.

Chapter 6

Now, I'll be honest, I know I wasn't the easiest child to raise. I had defiance of authority issues which wasn't a hit with my teachers, so I was always getting into trouble at school. I talked back. I always had a smart mouth. Still do (*flips hair*). I got into fights with my brothers, who both had very strong personalities. I got into fights with the boys on the playground, but they had it coming, always picking on me and whatnot...I regret nothing! I stole money from a vending machine at the Boys and Girls club and lied about it like a typical child would do. Or was it candy? I don't even remember at this point, but I do remember having to scrub a certain number of tiles with a toothbrush. I had temper tantrums. Again, I will never deny my behavioral issues, but as I've said before, I have witnessed children who behaved in the same manner, even more terrible than I ever did, and I would always ask myself, was I this bad? Was I way worse to have caused the events that followed? I got spanked a lot. Popped in the mouth a lot. Had my mouth washed out with soap...a lot. But Dee wasn't the physical or mental abuse type, but she had the maternal death stare to end all death stares, which I would get often. At this point is when I remember having "extended stays" with other families or family members, two in particular. I was around 7 years of age at this point. I remember staying with a family from our church. They had kids around my age. I don't quite remember how long I was with them, but I remember sleeping in bunkbeds with the other children. The other family was my grandparents in Miami. They were always so kind to me. We would start the mornings off with un Cafecito con pan (a little cup of Cuban coffee with bread). They had a beautiful backyard with a huge gazebo and a hammock, my personal hideaway. They had huge magnolia trees that were so beautiful. I climbed them plenty of times. Do you even live in Florida if you don't also have an orange tree or two?

The fragrance of magnolia and orange will forever be imprinted on my mind. It brings back a good childhood memory. My grandmother was a great cook, and I enjoyed the Cuban food she would make. My grandfather was a pastor, so naturally, I spent most of my time at their church. Part of being a pastor is that your doors always remain open, so members of their flock were coming and going. I would sit at the dining room table with my little Cafecito, which was mostly milk, all up in grown folks' business, pretending like I wasn't only there to eat the bread and guava pastries that would come out when the company was here. I don't recall ever having issues with them and I wished they would have kept me permanently. But they were older, and their family wasn't aware at the time just how much Dee was struggling with me. Or so they say. Maybe if she had been honest, she could have gotten the help she so desperately needed. I spent quite a few months here on the first go-around. I believe it was over summer break, but school started again so I would make my way back to Tennessee.

Around this time, another major "incident" happened that would set future events into motion, and it involved my younger sister, Nani. As was told to me by Dee herself, this was the final straw as far as she was concerned that prompted her to take the drastic action that she took. My sister and I were playing in the bathtub, laughing and splashing. We were taking turns dunking each other's heads under water. I specifically remember her doing it to me, but Dee just so happened to walk in when it was my turn to dunk her head in. Now looking back, I can see why this was so dangerous for us to be doing in the first place. Something catastrophic could have occurred if one of us held each other down just a little too long. I fully acknowledge that this wasn't the smartest or the safest game to be playing. We both were reprimanded, hosed down with cold water, and sent to bed without dinner. Both of us. There was not a single ounce of ill intent. From what I remember, we both were doing it and laughing the whole time. I tried to ask my sister in our adult life if she remembered this specific event so we could compare stories, but she was too young, about 6 years old. My sister and I, at this point in our lives were so close. We loved each other. I would have never wished for any harm towards her. Did we bicker and fight like sisters? I'm sure we did. Even though I was 11 months older than her, did I live in her shadow because she was the outgoing, lovable one? Yes. Did I act any differently towards her? No. Absolutely not. Looking back, I can see why Dee was so eager to get me out of the house. From what she witnessed, I just tried to murder my own sister.

The thing about being the black sheep of the family, the problem child, is that your word is taken with a grain of salt. Something untoward happens, and your suspect #1 and convicted without trial. There were 3 other children in the home, yet I got blamed for a lot of things. Food in the fridge missing? Blame the 7-year-old problem child even though there were 2 growing pre-teen boys in the house. Mysterious bruises on your siblings? Blame the problem child even though my brothers would get in literal fist fights. Hit me and my sister, too, but did I ever say anything? No, because who would believe me anyway? A case of inappropriate touching that makes my skin crawl to this day? I kept my mouth shut because who was going to. Believe. Me. Anyway? Boys will be boys after all. Something similar happened between my eldest brother and me. He shot me, point blank, with a bb gun. He swore up and down; he thought it was empty. I still have a scar on my right shoulder. Admittingly, it was a bb gun, but what if it had been to my face or my eyes? Maybe my head even. That could have caused some damage to a small child. But no one declared him insane or slapped him with a case of malicious intent. I didn't know this at the time, but after the incident with my sister, Dee sought out help from my case worker. She apparently declared me a danger to others and gave Dee two choices: institutionalize me or take me to a group home. She picked the lesser of two evils and chose the group home because she didn't want the stigma of being in a mental hospital to follow me for the rest of my life. How thoughtful... So off to the group home I went...

Chapter 7

I will state the obvious: I hated it here. I still consider the 2ish years I spent at this group home as some of the darkest and lowest points of my life. There wasn't anything wrong with the home in itself. From what I remember, the facilities were very clean (I should know because all the children that lived there had chores they had to do), and the faculty, for the most part, was really nice and seemed to care. I was told by my adoptive parents that I would only be here for a year to learn how to behave. Once that year was up and if I was a good girl, I would return home to my family. Challenge Accepted! I mean, I guess I didn't really have a choice in the matter. I met with a counselor once a week. She was super pretty; she almost reminded me of Snow White. She had pale skin and short black hair. She also had a stutter. I specifically remember thinking she was too pretty to have to deal with such things. We would play with toys, and she would ask me questions. My favorite was playdough and these little green dinosaurs. The Home, at the time, was faith-based and owned by a church that sat on the property, so we were forced to attend services on Wednesdays and Sundays. I was accustomed to attending church but there was something about this one that would put me to sleep. I got into trouble a lot because my head would be bobbing up and down, or I would just doze off. The highlight for me, though, was that once they found out I was musically inclined, I would go to weekly piano lessons, which would become the highlight of my stay here. We lived in cottages, separated by age groups and gender. My first cottage was with the youngest girls, I want to say ranging from about 6 to 13 or 14 years of age. When I got there, I was 8 years old and only remember a few girls that were younger than me coming and going. Some girls were there temporarily, only having to be there because a family member was being investigated or had to clear protocols to be able to get their children back. I knew this because my new suitemates would tell me. Others were there permanently, having been taken away from unfit parents or just in the foster care system longer-term.

We had a cycle of cottage parents who were in charge of us. They escorted us to the dining hall on the weekdays and cooked dinner on the weekends. They made sure we did our assigned chores and homework. They also would watch us take our medications if we were on any. I was still on ADHD medication. They had separate sleeping quarters on one side of the cottage and had a counter that reminded me of one of the counters you would see in doctor's offices, and we would line up, get handed our little cups with our pills in them, and had to show our mouths to make sure we swallowed them. Each child would receive a weekly score from 1 to 5 stars, 1 being very bad and 5 being very good. The cottage parents would base the score on how well we were behaving, how we were doing in school, if we completed our chores, how we were getting along with our cottage mates, etc.

I mostly stayed around 3 stars, so I was allowed to go to the gymnasium to play sports and mingle with the other cottage kids. This was the only few times that boys and girls would inter-mingle other than at church. I'm not going to lie; I had my little boyfriend I would see there. We would play basketball and sit on the bleachers. If you received 4-5 stars in the week, you would get to go on special field trips. I was only in this category twice, I believe. One trip was bowling, and the other trip was Dollywood! For the first year, I did alright. The biggest issue was school. I still talked back to teachers, and the boys still decided to pick on me, which would not go unpunished. I also got made fun of because I was one of the "group home" kids. Because of this, I would refuse to get off at our assigned bus stop because all the normal kids would see, and that landed me in hot water. I also have always been the type to bully my bullies right back but of course, the retaliators seem to get punished more than the aggressors. Plus, I already had a massive black mark against me, being that I, indeed, was one of the "group home" kids which automatically deemed me problematic. I have always enjoyed making my peers laugh, but sometimes I got in trouble for it. I was famous for my shadow puppets I would do at night, but they often kept us up past our curfew or making excessive noise.

I got along with my cottage parents for the most part in the beginning. Two specifically stuck out to me. One was this little Indian woman who was just as tall as some of the older girls, but she was fierce and stern, and we didn't mess with her. She would always wear these colorful sarees and had a bindi mark in between her eyes. She made the best-fried rice with eggs, carrots, and other vegetables. They were only responsible for cooking for us on weekends, but I always got excited when it was her weekend because of her delicious meals. The other one was a younger couple. They were super nice, and many times, I wished they were my parents. Again, the staff here were great for the most part.

The issues that arose during my first year were with certain children at the group home. When sexual assault and harassment happens between children, it isn't taken as seriously as it should be. You can sum it up to curiosity or children emulating the behavior that they've seen adults do or what they've seen on tv. In my mind, it makes it worse because we cannot fully comprehend what is happening. All I know is how it made me feel. I didn't know that what I was feeling at the time was shame and guilt. To me, it didn't feel good. I didn't like it. I wanted it to stop, but I had enough awareness to know that it was wrong and could get me in trouble. I was trying to be a good girl, remember? That way, I could go home soon. Plus, who would believe me anyway? Here we go with that same old feeling again. So, I let it happen. I didn't fight back. I didn't report it to my counselor or my cottage parents. There was one time I had had enough and was going to tell my cottage mom but was confronted at school about it. The group-home kids started spreading lies about me, and trust me, that didn't go over well in my little 9-year-old brain. That ended up with me in even more fights and altercations at school, which was doing nothing but damaging my case to be able to go home soon. So here I was, forced back into submission because all I wanted to do was go home. Now more than ever. I continued, going through the motions, trying my best not to get in trouble because my year was almost up. From a young age, I have always possessed the capacity to look on the bright side. To focus on the good things instead of the bad and that's what I did. I focused on my weekly piano lessons at the church and my gymnasium time with the other kids. Those were the two things I enjoyed most. I had friends at the gym and of course, my little boyfriend. I was active and have always been competitive. We had multiple staff members watching us at all times naturally, but one took a particular liking to me. He was sporty and cool and wore sunglasses inside, which we made fun of him for. He was always very nice and kind to me and asked me how I was doing, which I of course, never answered truthfully. He would also greet me at the dining hall as well. He genuinely seemed to care. Now, my only issue with him is that he would always put his hands on my shoulders and give me hugs, which I never really saw him do to the other children. Once, he placed his hand on the small of my back, which sent shivers down my spine. Let me make one thing clear, he never inappropriately touched me. I never saw him outside of the dining hall, gym, or field trips. In fairness, to this day, I still hate when people rub, squeeze, or place their hands on my shoulders. I have been sexually assaulted and inappropriately touched in my lifetime.

I shouldn't have to explain why I don't want to be touched like that, but I have had to do so many times, even as an adult. Most people find the gesture harmless, and in most cases, it is. I can't help how it makes me feel. I made the unfortunate mistake of telling my counselor about how Mr. So-n-So would squeeze my shoulders and that I didn't like how it made me feel. Suddenly, I never went to gym-time anymore. I never saw the nice man again, either. I am not sure what happened to him, but as a child, I never pieced together how a comment like that could have been taken and the consequences it would cause.

So, my first year was coming to a close. Trust me, I was keeping track. I was excited to leave this place. Excited to be back home with a family I thought loved me. Excited to get back to a normal life and not be branded as one of the problematic "group home" kids at school. Some of the girls from my cottage went home for visits with their families. Mine visited me once or twice in the span of a year, but I never had an overnight visit or taken home for the weekend. They didn't even come up for my birthday. I did receive a card though. My sister was growing up without me, and I felt it. We weren't thick as thieves anymore. No one ever seemed excited to see me. Not my brothers. Not my adoptive father. Most certainly not my adoptive mother. We went to Dollywood once as a family. That was cool. Dollywood is an interesting place with all things Dolly Parton and wooden rollercoasters. I was anxious! I was antsy! I was eager to blow this popsicle stand! The year finally ended, and I was waiting for my family to pick me up any moment finally. I was still going to my weekly meeting with my counselor, but this particular meeting was different. This meeting was with a woman I had never met before. She had long, light brown hair and rimmed glasses. She took me into a room I also had never been in before. And that is when it happened. This woman, this stranger, broke the news to me that there had been a change of plans. I was going to stay in the group home until I was 18 years old. After that, since I'd technically be an adult, I could go wherever I wanted. My adoptive parents didn't even have the audacity to tell me this news themselves. Something inside me was completely broken. What was left of my innocence dissipated into thin air. The little flickering light that I was trying so hard to keep lit within me was completely blown out, and I was left in complete darkness.

I was numb at first, trying to make sense of everything that had happened. It hadn't hit my little 9-year-old brain what it truly all meant. What it truly would have meant to stay there for another 9 years. I was already having a hard time in elementary school. I could have only imagined what middle and high school would have been like with the bullying. I had been given up on. I no longer had a family. I could say goodbye to happy Christmases and themed birthday parties. Sleepovers with friends and trying out for sports teams. Mother-daughter spa days or crying in her arms during my first puppy love heartbreak. I always felt protective over my little sister, but who was going to look after her now? She was already growing up without me, and now it was made permanent. The only family that I truly had was taken away from me. I was utterly alone in this life. The numbness soon passed, and all that was left was anger and pain that blossomed into full-on rage. I will admit that for the next year, I was an absolute terror, the villain that I was painted to be. All I had left was my pain. How was a 9-year-old girl supposed to cope with so many emotions, emotions I might add, that she didn't even understand? I was hurting, and who was there to comfort me but my own demons? My own suffering? I lashed out at anyone who crossed my path. I no longer had to be a "good girl," so I could go home and no one could tell me anything. The things that I let happen to me never happened again because I fought back now. At this point, I had nothing left to lose. I scared them enough to leave me alone. All my privileges had been taken away. No piano lessons. No seeing my friends at the gymnasium. No extra field trips. I had completely given up on life and was adamant about taking it.

Now, I was on suicide watch and prescribed an anti-depressant on top of my ADHD medication. I was now deemed a danger to myself as well as others. I had to switch cottages because I kept getting into fights with my cottage mates, and the cottage parents couldn't handle me. I was switched to one more of the same age group, but the same thing happened so my last option was the cottage with the teenage girls. At least I had my own room, and they left me alone for the most part because I was 10 and still a holy terror. I did have some peace here, though, at least for a bit. I was allowed to keep my little radio player that never parted from my ears. My favorite song was Brian McKnight's "Back at One" and I would listen to the radio in hopes they would play it again and again. I find that amusing because headphones rarely part from my ears to this day as a 34-year-old woman. Music has always kept the voices away...and I am dead serious when I say that.

The beginning of the end at the group home shortly followed. I was so bad at school that I was expelled. I would refuse to take my medications because they made me feel funny, so it became almost a daily occurrence that I would have a grown man literally pin down my arms, and a grown woman straddle me and force pills down my throat. The thing about being in the teenager's cottage is that they had more privileges, like Walmart trips to buy clothes and makeup. Some of them would steal eyeshadows and lipstick, and I, of course, was at a very impressionable age and did the same, except I wasn't as good as them and got caught. One girl in the cottage started bullying me, and my old instincts kicked back in, and I started getting into fights with a 17-year-old. My suitemate was super nice, though, and would stand up for me. Her name was Lisa, and I remember her being super pretty with blonde hair and blue eyes. She had a thick country accent; it was Tennessee, after all. She liked me because since her boyfriend was Black, she said that she hoped their kids would look like me. She was the big sister I would never have. She was also 17, close to aging out, and would constantly talk about the future. College was out of the question, but she planned on getting a job and moving in with her boyfriend. I don't remember her story if she told me to begin with. I think of her often because what actually happens to the children that age out of the system? But I'll talk about that later. The thing is, there wasn't another cottage I could be moved to if I couldn't manage to get along with the teenage cottage mates, which I eventually ended up not being able to do, of course. So here I was, expelled from school, causing problems everywhere they put me. And then it happened one April. I was somehow going home for Easter and asked not to return. According to both my adoptive mother and the woman I call my mom, I was the first child in the history of that group home to have ever gotten kicked out. I was that bad...

Chapter 8

The Lajas's were stuck with me again and running out of options. I could tell I wasn't welcome. They had since moved into another house in a nice neighborhood. There wasn't an extra room for me, so I slept on a daybed in the upstairs hallway. Dee had told me that she didn't want to put me in the same room with my sister because of the "sexual activity" that had happened at the group home. I never wanted to deck someone in the face as much as I wanted to in that moment. She never once asked for my side of the story. She never once consoled me because I was the victim here. She never once cared. I'm sorry, but despite what she might have said, her actions, time and again, showed me differently. I was locked out of the house a lot for hours at a time to play outside and find something to keep myself occupied. They had a swing set in the backyard, and so I would sit until I was allowed to come back inside. I don't remember that happening to the other 3 kids in the house, so naturally, I found it suspicious. I wasn't in school.

I actually never finished the 4th grade. I was shipped off yet again to my grandparents in Miami for a time. I didn't mind it though; like I said before, I really wished my grandparents would have just kept me permanently. I took a Greyhound bus to Miami, and my Godfather accompanied me. It was nice talking to him, and we bonded during this trip. I was comfortable with him because I didn't feel judged. He was the black sheep of his family too, so how could he? I felt loved there. I felt wanted and cared for. I didn't feel like a burden or excess baggage. This time around, one of my male cousins was there as well, and we had grown close. I had a true friend. It saddens me to this day that out of all my adoptive relatives, he wasn't the one who kept in contact. But of course, my stay here was never permanent. I would eventually make it back to Tennessee one last time. I was 11 years old then. All I remember from this day is waking up to an empty house. It was just me and Dee. My siblings weren't there, and neither was my adoptive father. Dee sat me down at the dining room table and gave me an ultimatum: either I was to go with this other family permanently, or I'd be kicked out on the street. Great, homeless at 11 years of age. To me, it was a no-brainer, although the decision had already been made for me. My stuff was already packed and the family in question were already on their way and would be at the house any moment. I was completely beside myself, but deep down, I wasn't surprised. I never was able to say goodbye to my sister. Not that I expected the rest of the Lajas clan to care, but it did hurt my feelings that no one even bothered to say their farewells. I hadn't even stayed with them a full year before I was rehomed again, like a fucking dog, except most dogs get treated better. And just like that, my journey as a Lajas would come to an end.

Chapter 9

When I reflect on the moments spent with the Lajas family, I can't help but feel angry. For the longest time, that anger consumed me, and it was so evident. I truly believe that some of us are born with a more natural capacity for rage. A fire lit at all times, just bubbling beneath the surface. If that fire goes unchecked, it does what fire does: destroy everything in its path. I will be the first to admit that I live with this fire every single day. This chapter of my life is a reminder of what happens when I can't control it and just how self-destructive I can be; mind you, I was 9 years of age at the time. But I also can't deny that Dee's actions fanned an already unstable flame. Is it wrong of me to think that despite everything that happened, I still hold myself blameless? I was a child, admittingly, a difficult one, but a child, nonetheless. A child who already felt the sting of abandonment. A child who already felt unloved and unwanted. Why further that pain by cutting into wounds that hadn't even begun to heal? Were her actions any different than what I had already experienced? Was I even given the opportunity to feel safe, to feel like I had a home to finally start the healing process anyway? No, I wasn't. Why would she, in turn, expect me to act any differently? Now, one can say that I was the prime example as to why families do not want to adopt older children, but how much blame can one put on a 5-year-old? Why must the innocents be the ones to reap the consequences of circumstances entirely out of their control? We are the victims but rarely are we treated as such. I was villainized before I even reached their doorstep. Remember, my sister and I had to get adopted together. Dee had told me on multiple occasions that they wanted to adopt both of us, but her actions proved what I knew to be true. She was so quick to cast me away from the beginning. Let's do a quick timeline recap. I was adopted at 5 and in a group home by 8. Kicked out of the group home at 10 and rehomed by 11. So that leaves about 4 years I actually spent with the Lajas's, but let's not forget the multiple times I was left with random families and the months I spent with my grandparents, not a lot of time at all.

I am going to compare myself to a shelter dog for a moment, so go with me on this. Most dog lovers preach the whole notion of "adopt don't shop" meaning there are so many shelter dogs that need loving homes instead of giving your money to puppy mills. Some shelter dogs get adopted quickly because they are cute and energetic and bond with people naturally. Those dogs acclimate to the home instantly and seamlessly become a part of the family. Other shelter dogs are skittish, get aggressive when you try to pet them or don't even bother to engage. In most cases, those dogs were abused, neglected, or have been rehomed multiple times. Are you starting to see the parallels? When these types of shelter dogs get adopted, their transition into the home may take some time. They display the same type of behavior at first: skittish, distant, maybe aggressive if you come too close but with some TLC, they start to warm up to their new owners. They start to engage more. They eventually become playful and loving and start to show more of their personalities. They realize that this family has their best interest at heart. They are here to feed them, love them, and give them all the cuddles (clearly, I'm a dog person myself.) This process could take weeks, maybe even months, but the important thing is patience and consistency. What you don't do is display the same type of behavior that made them the way they are, to begin with. You don't combat aggressive and distant behavior with more aggressive behavior. This makes them act worse. These types of shelter dog success stories tug at the heart strings because people took a chance on the dog who was rough around the edges. Who had been overlooked so many times before and chose to show love to the ones who needed it the most. Now, humans are way more complex than our canine friends, but the concept is the same, isn't it? I constantly wonder how differently things might have turned out had I been shown more love and compassion rather than being treated like a disease, an infection you couldn't wait to be rid of. I was never really given a proper chance to be a part of their family. I wasn't perfect, but neither were the other children in the house. I eventually grew out of my behavioral issues to become the lovely yet still imperfect person I am today. Why couldn't they have had just a little more patience with me? I graduated in the top 10% of my class in high school. I have a bachelor's degree. Despite everything, I made something of myself and barely scratched the surface of what I am meant to do. I turned out ok, better than ok even.

The next time I saw the Lajas family was when I was 14 years old. My new family was hesitant to take me to see them because they were afraid they'd want me back now that I was "normal." It was a pleasant enough visit, and I will admit, I was hoping they'd want me back. I wanted them to see how well I was doing what they gave up on. I was eager to show them that I wasn't the little girl who was starving for their love and acceptance anymore. I was also hoping that they'd save me from the current nightmare they forced me to endure, but that story is coming later. What ended up happening was that I was a stranger. Again, no one was that excited to see me, not even my sister, who would have been 13 at the time. We weren't close anymore. We seldom kept in contact, but Dee did send pictures from time to time. I was still an imposter, although it was said they did try to get me back, but I knew it was simply too late. They had been receiving government checks on my behalf, even the times I didn't live with them, and my new mom threatened to report them if they tried. That was her go-to threat when they got out of line which worked like a charm every time. That was something that bothered me immensely because they would have received those checks until college, which would have helped me a lot.

I was basically on my own and responsible for myself since I was 18. My new parents tried their best, but they didn't have money like that. Dee said they soon had the checks stopped after this visit because of my new mom's threat, but I don't believe that for a second because wouldn't that have raised several questions? Like where was I? What happened to me? Why did they continue to claim those checks all the times prior when I hadn't lived in the home for years? That's the big one.

I didn't have contact with any of my adoptive family after that until college. The invention of Facebook came along around that time as well, and my adoptive cousins and extended family started adding me like crazy. I did for a time, have my adoptive family on Facebook too, at least Dee and my two brothers. My new family never got around to adopting me, so I was still legally, a "Lajas" so I think the relatives were simply adding everyone with that specific surname. It was nice for a time. To see them growing up and becoming mothers, husbands, and wives. My younger cousins, who were in diapers when I left, were now grown and flourishing. Both my God parents had gotten married and had families of their own. I missed out on so much. The holiday photos were the thing that got to me the most. They were a big family but still managed to get together for Thanksgiving and/or Christmas. Holidays haven't been the same since and are always a reminder of dark times in my life. One Christmas around my sophomore year of college, I was lurking as I typically did around that time of year and saw something that shook me to my core. My adoptive family posted their annual family Christmas photo. There were a few new faces, the significant others of my brothers, and a few grandchildren. But one face in particular was missing: my sister. I never interacted with any of them online. I didn't like pictures. I didn't share posts. But I was overcome in that moment and commented under this photo, *"Where's Nani?"* Of course, I never got a reply, but throughout the comment section of other relatives saying how beautiful a family they were and to have a Merry Christmas, I saw a relative I had never met before ask them who I was. *"Who is Lauren Lajas?"* I was livid. All those feelings came back to the surface, and I was a cloud of darkness for a while after that. My sister wasn't on Facebook yet that I could find, and I was never given a method of contact for her. My mind was racing with what could have possibly happened. I was also upset that I wasn't even acknowledged. She was MY family too, and I had a right to know how she was doing. I always wondered what the explanation was as to my disappearance anyway. How did those dinner conversations go? Was I removed from the family portraits? When I suddenly stopped showing up at the family functions, was anyone not the least bit curious as to why? In a fit of rage and sadness, I deleted every single relative off my Facebook. Who was I kidding? I was never a part of that family. I was causing myself grief living in a fantasy that they still saw me as such. In truth, I wanted them to see how great I was doing. I was in college and in a sorority. I had a lot of friends. The braces were close to coming off, and I lost a bunch of weight. I was feeling good about myself. But none of those things made them see me. None of those things made them want to reach out and be a part of my life. I was brought back to that little girl, starving for love and wanting a family. I was filled with a sense of worthlessness and thinking that no matter what I did and how much I changed, I would never be good enough, so I was done. Done pretending. Done letting them have such a stronghold on my emotions and self-worth. I was never going to be invited to the cookout or made a God parent to one of my nieces or nephews. I was never going to be asked to be in one of their bridal parties or be close enough to ask them to be in mine. I was never going to wear matching pajamas sets with them on Christmas. I had to let these fantasies go. I read somewhere once that you sometimes have to acknowledge the part you play in your own suffering. It was time to rip off the band aid. To open the floodgates and feel all those emotions I suppressed for so long. No one died, but I felt the loss anyway. I let myself mourn them; then I let them go for good.

The only adoptive relative that has reached out a few times in my life was my God mother. She noticed that I had deleted her off Facebook and messaged me that she was sad, but she understood. I won't lie; I let her have it. How could she possibly understand? How could she understand what It feels like to be thrown away like garbage? To be rehomed so many times, I've lost count. And for none of them to care. So much for family. She then told me that when Dee's family found out about what she had done to me, they were furious and stopped talking to her for a time. They wanted to know where I was so they could come and get me. The thing is, they never did. I never received phone calls, birthday cards, or letters from anyone. The intent might have been there, but the actions weren't. She gave me an update on my sister as well. She had hit a rough patch with her parents, and they did what they do, send her away to some program out of state. I will admit that at the time, I wasn't mature enough to have this conversation. I was very closed-off and only saw my own pain. That night, I stayed up tossing and turning. I was so upset with all of them. How could they live with themselves for doing the same thing to her as they did to me? Just discard her away. How do they sleep at night? All of a sudden, a voice popped into my head that said, *"Don't worry how they sleep at night. Worry how you sleep at night."* The voice of God in my head is a sassy black man, like a Billy Porter or a Lafayette Reynolds from True Blood.

I looked up at my ceiling, a.k.a. God, at that moment and scoffed. I laid in my bed, annoyed, but deep down, I knew he was right. I needed to be concerned with how I was sleeping. I was the one tossing and turning, not them. That famous quote came to mind, you know the one. The one that says, "holding onto anger is like drinking poison and expecting the other person to die." That was me. I was holding onto so much anger and animosity that I was only hurting myself. I chose to work on letting go for my sake. But also, I have done things in my life that have kept others up at night. I couldn't pass judgment when I too, could be judged.

Chapter 10

Moment of Truth…

In January of 2021, it was placed upon my heart to start my media company. I was going to start with my own projects which would implement a blog, dating podcast, original music, and a YouTube Series. Why yes, I am doing a lot. In May of that same year, I released one of my first videos in celebration of Mother's Day. I discussed the relationships I had with my mothers to shed light on the fact that while for most, Mother's Day is a joyous occasion to celebrate the leading ladies in our lives, it isn't for all of us. For some of us, it is filled with sadness and regret. Dee somehow saw this video and decided to message me on the good old Facebook. She told me that she saw my video and that if I had any questions, I only had to ask. Mind you, I hadn't had contact with her since I was 15 years old. I was now 31. It took me some time to wrap my head around what was happening. But after I gathered my thoughts and calmed myself down, my first question was why she put me in the group home, why she decided to keep me there, and then why she gave me away yet again after the group home. Why? WHY? That is when I found out it was either that or institutionalize me due to being deemed a danger to others. She had to look out for her own family, including my sister. That and I had threatened to burn the house down with everyone inside on multiple occasions. Personally, I don't remember saying that, but given my fascination with fire and fondness for matches in my youth, I wouldn't have put it past me. Ouch. That was very hard to hear. The irony in that statement was many times in my younger years; I wanted to throw in the towel and commit myself. Let them lock me up in a padded room and throw away the key. Sometimes, life was just too much to bear. My inner demons would torment me relentlessly, and...sometimes my own anger did scare me. Maybe it would have been best if I was locked away. One of those points was when I was told that I'd be staying at the group home until I was 18, and the year of holy terror followed. I didn't have a textbook mental breakdown, but something broke in me that day. The other times, I'll get to soon. At 31 years of age, this was the first time she was willing to hear my side of the story. First time. She wasn't aware of what actually went on at the group home, that I was a victim. That her decision to leave me there made me spiral out of control. I was doing ok before then. I wasn't perfect, but I wasn't wreaking havoc like I did my second year there. Which I will never deny. According to Dee, one of the reasons I was kicked out was that I was also threatening sexual abuse allegations towards the staff, which wasn't how that conversation happened at all. That was disappointing to hear. She regretted it all. Lamented how if I believed in karma, she was paying for it. At this point, she had had two heart attacks, was in a wheelchair due to a diabetic amputation, and her own family fell apart. My two brothers couldn't stand the sight of each other, and they even had separate visits for the holidays. They haven't been a happy family for a while. I have learned to only be concerned with my own karma, so I didn't have much to say about that. One thing that struck me as odd was that she was saddened at the fact that I never chose to keep in contact. As she put it, communication is a two-way street. My adoptive family often asked about me, but slowly, they stopped because I never reached out to them either. That statement sent me. I had to take some time before I replied. We had to agree to disagree with that one. Why would I reach out first? I was the black sheep. The pariah. The problem child. Life is made up of choices; they could have chosen to keep in contact. I didn't know what was said about me and how they felt about the entire situation. I think that was her guilt talking because in what universe would I have been the one to reach out? For decades, I thought these people hated me. She also stated that she wished that I would have come to see her as a second mother. I think she was looking for a friend. An escape from the situation she created possibly. That statement broke my heart because, in my mind, it was simply too late. I was a grown woman in her 30s now. I had lost the person I called my mom a few years prior to this, and I couldn't let myself fall for that fantasy yet again. That part of my heart was permanently closed. Truth be told, I didn't know how to be what she wanted without it breaking me. Even in a simple conversation over Facebook, I was being brought back to that broken little girl, still starving for something I would never have. I couldn't do that to myself. Not at this age. Not when I've come so far. And a part of me was cynical. She didn't deserve to know me now that I was funny, charismatic, and an overall beautiful person. I left the conversation that I'd try my best to stay in contact, but I didn't. I couldn't.

The next time I would talk to Dee was in August of 2023. I had decided to move to Denver, Colorado, from Florida and was taking the scenic route through Tennessee. One of my pitstops was Gatlinburg. My gut was telling me that she didn't have long to live, so it was now or never to make my peace. I also wanted to do a segment on the group home I stayed in, which ironically was on the way as well. The Smokey Mountains were a wonder to behold. I hadn't seen them since I was a child. I enjoyed the crisp freshness of the mountain air and took in its majestic beauty. I have made Colorado my home but if I had to choose, Smokies all the way! A creek was just outside my balcony of the hotel, and I would sit out there and listen to the water trickling down the hill. The sound of rushing water has always brought me peace. I think that's why I love the ocean so much. Hearing the waves crash upon the shore brings me to a place of tranquility. I traded in sharks and alligators for bears and saw them a little too close for comfort a few times. I treated myself to a solo tubing trip and made my way down the river. Of course, I missed the clearing I was supposed to get off at and had to get off my tube and swim against the current to the nearest clearing. Admittedly, it was a humbling experience. I fancy myself a decent swimmer, but I was under-prepared for the depth of the water against a very strong current. It was touch and go there for a moment or two, but it was awesome! The calm before the metaphorical storm. The next day, I made my way to the group home. It was owned by the state now, so the name changed, but everything else was just as I remembered it. I knew I wouldn't be able to set up a camera on the property, but I had found a gazebo across the street. I set up the tripod and put on my mic. I took one last glance at my pocket mirror. Alright, I was ready. Lights! Camera! Action! I was overwhelmed with emotions and broke down crying within seconds. Dammit, would I ever be over this place? This chapter of my life? I gave myself a few moments to stop crying before I tried again with the same result. It just wasn't time yet to share my story. It had been over 20 years, so I knew none of the staff there would remember me or even work there, but I made my way to the main hall. I wanted to ask for my file anyway. I spoke to a nice gentleman who was shocked that I was there. As one can imagine, it wouldn't be the first destination we'd choose to come visit. He was glad to see that I was doing well and looked me up on YouTube to listen to my music, and wanted a copy of the book I was writing when I finished it. He took down my information and told me that if they could find my file, he'd send me a copy. I've asked twice with no such luck. It was time for me to leave and make my way to Pigeon Forge, where I'd be meeting my adoptive parents. They lived a few hours away but said they'd make the drive to meet me when I told them I'd be in the area, which I appreciated. They hadn't physically seen me in 19 years. Again, I was a grown woman now. They were both in wheelchairs as my adoptive father had started dialysis for his ailments. We met at a little Cuban café on the strip. Leave it to them to find the only Cuban restaurant in the area! The conversation wasn't awkward. I gave myself a huge peptalk before I walked into the café to be cordial and not defensive. I was very proud of myself that I wasn't. I was pleasant enough, giving them the cliff notes version of my life for the past few decades. College graduate. No kids. No boyfriend (they were shocked at that revelation). Lived in LA to pursue music. Moving to Denver to further along my creative pursuits and live near one of my closest friends. They did the same. Giving me updates on their grandchildren and what my brothers were up to. They recapped the drama between them. Both my brothers were gifted musicians and chose opposite career paths in the arts. My eldest brother was in a band, and the younger one was a band teacher. He was also sickly as well, having had multiple heart attacks when he was only a few years older than I was. They hadn't heard from my sister in a while so no update there. Unfortunately, neither had I so I didn't have anything to report either. But now to the reason as to why I wanted to see them. I wanted to acknowledge the fact that I now realize that it couldn't have been easy to make the decisions they made concerning me. I made it abundantly clear that I felt like they were the wrong decisions nevertheless, but that I forgave them. They did the best they could, and despite everything, I turned out ok. Dee told me not to blame my adoptive father, that he never wanted to give me away and wanted no part in those decisions, which made sense as to why he wasn't there when the final act happened. He didn't stop anything though, so in my mind, that statement was hollow, but I wasn't there to argue. They appreciated my maturity, bringing up multiple times how difficult I was back then, which I again acknowledged. I would then reiterate that despite my difficulties, the situation was not handled properly and could have been handled better. This would somehow be brought back to how difficult I was, which I would AGAIN acknowledge that I understood that. However, better decisions could have been made. I realized then that I was not going to receive the closure I was looking for. I just wanted them to admit that they messed up. That the decisions they chose to make weren't the right ones and that they were sorry. That is all I wanted to hear. Deep down, I knew that this conversation was more for their benefit. They needed to hear that I forgave them. I did my part. And I would have to accept the apology I would never get and move on. They wanted to know when I arrived in Denver, and I texted them when I made it so they knew I made it safely. 4 months later, Dee passed away. I mourned for her years ago, so I wasn't as torn up about it, and I don't think anyone expected me to be. And just like that, this chapter of my life was closed.

Chapter 11

I didn't know Dee all that well. I wasn't given a chance to. If you remember the timeline, I was only with the Lajas family for around 4 years. I truly believe they didn't give me enough time to adjust. They were overwhelmed and panicked. She seemed to always want to deflect responsibility. It wasn't her decision to take me to the home. It wasn't her decision to have me stay there until I was 18. It wasn't her decision to want to dump me on her family every chance she got. It was never her fault. Of course, I have my opinions on the matter, but she did remind me that she was making decisions on the fly at the age that I am now. 34 years of age. I wonder to myself, would I have acted any differently? I like to think I would have, knowing what I now know, but who's to say? I really try to have some compassion. I know deep down it couldn't have been easy. Like I said at the beginning of my book, when adults make mistakes, it's the children that suffer for it. And I suffered immensely. I am a 34-year-old woman, and I still get brought to tears when I think about this time of my life. I still have sleepless nights when my mind decides to take a journey down memory lane. I still feel the need to self-isolate at times because I feel numb to the world, and I don't think it's fair to the people around me to have to deal with me when I'm like that. I also feel alone and so misunderstood, but I hope the people closest to me would be the first to read my book to maybe gain some understanding as to why I am the way that I am. I do bounce back rather quickly because the show must go on. But childhood trauma stays with you forever. It just manifests in different ways. But I have matured enough to know that while I wasn't the one who inflicted these traumas, I am responsible for how I let it affect me now. I couldn't blame Dee forever. One of the last things she told me was that I choose to hold on to the bad memories when there were good ones as well. My response to that has always been when the bad memories far outweigh the good; it is very hard to focus on the good. I can try to convince my mind to focus on the Disney trips and the birthday parties, but my heart weighs heavy. Oh, so heavy. I can't control the nightmares and the restlessness. I was suicidal as a 9-year-old. I didn't want to live anymore, and my life was only beginning.

I would have loved an opportunity to be her daughter. We could have bonded over our creativity. I am a girly tomboy, meaning while I love sports and can talk shop with the boys, I also love fashion, skincare, and makeup. You know, girly stuff! I am insightful and wise beyond my years. Our conversations would have been meaningful. As I said with my biological mother, I don't know what my life would have looked like had I stayed and grown up in the Lajas household. Would I be the version of myself that I am today? Would I have the same passions? Would I have the same fire I have for domestic violence and foster care awareness? Would I have discovered my gift of songwriting in the manner that I did? I will never know, and again, I choose not to dwell on those fantasies. I can say, again, that I wouldn't change a thing because I know I survived. I made it to this version of myself, and I wholeheartedly love her. I love how passionate and fiery I am. I will never apologize for being that way. I learned to control my fire and use it for something meaningful and purposeful. In truth, I consider being made aware of the capacity I have for violence and self-destruction at a very young age a blessing. The older you get, the harder it is to break habits and patterns of behavior. We all know this. Having that type of unchecked rage and disregard for authority has way more life-altering consequences as an adolescent or even going into adulthood. I was the stereotypical foster child. Meaning what was expected of me was to end up dead in a ditch somewhere, on drugs, or in jail. And my anger would have been the catalyst.

One of the biggest reasons I am able to "tame the storm within," so to speak, is because of music and creativity. What I am most grateful for is that Dee gave me a purpose, whether she knew it or not. She exposed me to the world of singing, and for the first time in my life, I had found something that made me feel significant. It gave my life meaning. It set me apart and raised me above my pain. My past. The giant chip on my shoulder I had for years. When I would sing in church or made to sing for anyone and everyone that came to the house, for a few moments, I wasn't the delinquent. The ticking time bomb they were anticipating would explode at any moment. I was simply the little girl with such a lovely voice who could make the world go silent. The admiration in their eyes...it made me want to strive to be a different version of the child they knew. And that goal,

having an objective to put all my energy towards, changed my life. It didn't do either of us any good to hold on to the past. We both suffered in our own ways. But for me, choosing to hold a grudge against her or any of her family for that matter, will only hurt me. So, I'm letting it go. I'm choosing me. Something that, quite frankly, didn't happen a lot in my childhood. I'm choosing the memories I hold onto. I'm choosing to hold the opinion I have of myself above all others. I'm choosing my peace of mind.

My Mom

Chapter 12

Man, this is the hardest part of my story to tell. The next and last woman I am going to discuss was the woman I considered to be my mom. The woman who raised me through perhaps the hardest years: the adolescent period. She loved me, and I know that with every fiber of my being but, she too left massive scars on my heart. Inflicted both literal and figurative wounds that I'm still healing from to this day. Let's pick up where we left off shall we? So, at 11 years of age, I was now off with another family. My adoptive mother wasn't lying when she said they were on the way because, within the hour, they were there. They had driven from Florida to Tennessee in a taupe-colored van. When they got there, I remember my new parents crying when they saw me, which I found odd. I didn't know them, but they knew me. See, they were one of the foster parents I had before I got adopted, Ruthie and Ramon. The family that had tried to adopt me and my sister. They were overcome with emotions and started kissing and hugging me while I awkwardly stood there, still trying to process what was actually happening. Dee and my new mom had a brief discussion while my new dad put my belongings in the van. And just like that, I got into a minivan with complete strangers to start a new life. I don't remember too much of the ride back to Florida, except that it was a long one. My new parents regaled stories of when I was little and constantly repeated how God had answered their prayers to bring me back into their lives. I wasn't buying into this new fantasy of a happy home with parents who loved me, but they seemed nice enough, so I tried not to be a brat about the situation. We finally made it to my new home, where I tried to look on the bright side, but at this point, I was defeated. But hey, maybe this time, it would be different. A broken little girl could still dream, right?

A few changes were made from the beginning. Firstly, my new mom took me off the two medications I was taking because she said they made me a zombie. I was grateful for this because they still made me feel strange anyway. No more ADHD meds or antidepressants for me! Secondly, I had to get used to the fact that I was now in a religious household. Super religious. The first thing to go was my Walkman, my most prized possession. All my CDs and tapes were confiscated because, in this house, "secular" music wasn't allowed, so goodbye to my entire music collection. The Walkman had to go because I could still listen to the radio, which played the type of music that was now banned from my ears. How dare they! Well, at first, I was still allowed to listen to it as long as I listened to Christian stations, but I got caught too many times on other ones, so it was taken altogether. At random times, the headphones would be snatched from my ears, not giving me enough time to change the station back. Good times. A lot of my clothes were taken away as well. Apparently, wearing pants and shorts would send you to the deepest circles of Hell. That wouldn't do. I was given hand-me-downs, which wasn't the problem.

The problem was that the hand-me-downs that I was given weren't necessarily something an 11-year-old would wear. As I referred to them often, they were "old lady clothes." I tried to get used to my new life, which basically consisted of church. Tuesdays, Wednesdays, Thursdays, sometimes on Saturdays, and of course, on Sundays. Naturally, I protested every chance I got, but I learned that any form of disobedience was answered with a slap, punch, or aggressive tug of hair, clothing, or whatever could be grabbed at the moment. I quickly realized that my current situation wasn't going to be sunshine and rainbows. I hated church because we seemed to live there. The services were also in Spanish, barely my second language so I didn't understand a thing. I was also paraded around as the "miracle." The answered prayer of my new parents. Strangers would come up to me, telling their little anecdotes about how they knew me as a toddler. It was all too much for me at the time. My new mom was strict. Well, that was an understatement. I remained rebellious as ever. That was not a great mix, so discord was there from the beginning. What caused friction at first was that I refused to call my new mom, "mom." These weren't my parents. I already had parents, and they lived in another state. I was still under the impression that this situation was temporary. Clearly, I was delusional. The months rolled on, but I still had hope. It wasn't until I started school that I gave up. That and I would be completely ignored. I would not be acknowledged if I wasn't using "mom" and "dad." That got old fast, so I just gave in and started calling them by their wanted names.

5th grade, yay! I was glad that I didn't get held back a year because I never really finished the 4th grade. I had to take special tests that placed me at the "gifted" level, but all those classes were full, and so were the regular ones, so I was put in the remedial class. What a breeze. I had to take multiple tests to prove I understood English, which was odd to me, but clearly, I passed. Regular visits to the school counselor were, of course, mandatory for me, but those stopped when my counselor one time referred to my sister as my "half-sister," which upset my mom. I distinctly remember that conversation because my mom sat me down to explain to me that while my sister and I had different dads, that didn't make her any less my sister, which I never thought to begin with. But sure. Ok. Here I was at a new school, a fresh start. Except a week before school was supposed to start, I made the unfortunate mistake of going to bed with gum in my mouth that ended up in my hair. We had to cut it all off. That would be the perfect accessory to my granny clothing that I was still being forced to wear. What a great first impression. School was school. I continued to get bullied. The main reasons were because of, you guessed it, my hair and my outfits. I've been bullied because of my hair most of my life, so that didn't really phase me. They called me Treetop, Afro Thunder, and Opossum Head.

Opossum Head did kind of hurt my feelings because the kids said it looked like roadkill had died on my head. I have always had thick eyebrows, so the kids also said it looked like caterpillars had died on my face. The thing is, I was still in the habit of bullying them right back, so they had learned early on to leave me alone. One of my biggest bullies would end up being my best friend for the next few decades. The one that I would adamantly ask to change was my clothing. I couldn't do much about my hair until it grew out or my eyebrows, but the clothes, we could change. All I wanted was to feel normal. Of course, I was shot down. That's when the mental abuse started to kick in, being told that I was an ungrateful bitch and that I should be lucky that I had her because no one else wanted me. If it wasn't for her, I would be on the street and probably end up like my birth mother (remember, she was a drug addict and a prostitute). If I had a dollar every time I would hear that one the next decade of my life... She picked out my clothes for the longest, and I felt like she was doing it on purpose just to assert her authority. One time, I had to do something in front of the entire grade. I picked out an outfit that she would approve of: modest, not tight, and of course, a dress. I expressed how important it was to me because I was going to be in front of so many of my peers. She proceeded to pick out the outfit I hated the most just to teach me a lesson. I objected, pleading, just this once if I could wear the outfit I picked out. I was beaten this time. I had been hit and smacked before. My hair had been pulled. But this time, I was hit over and over, nose bleeding, with chunks of hair on my bathroom floor. Remember when I said there were a few times when I wanted to give up and commit myself to an institution? This was one of them. I was forced to sit in the tub until my nose stopped bleeding, and so I sat there, stunned. I was replaying what had just happened over and over in my mind, wondering how I might have managed to trade one nightmare in for another.

Chapter 13

Middle school came around, and I couldn't really say I was excited. I was struggling to acclimate to the rigid system that was my new life. I am naturally rebellious, so I fought it at every turn, which would lead to more beatings, but I didn't care. Following so many rules just doesn't come naturally to me, especially when the source was because the bible said so. The bible said I couldn't go to a friend's house. I couldn't go to the mall, the movies, or school dances because sin happens there. On the weekends, while my peers were making plans to go shopping or to the lake, I worked with my new dad. He had a small lawn care business, and I became his #1 employee. Well, his only employee. I spent this time cutting the grass, trimming hedges, picking up the clippings etc. My dad was a jack of all trades, so he installed kitchen cabinets, laid down tile and wood flooring, painting inside and out of homes, and more. Guess who his little helper was? Me. I didn't really mind it much. It was our father/daughter time.

That, and watching baseball. He had 6 daughters from other marriages, so I was the closest thing to a son he's ever had. I got used to not asking to make plans on the weekends because it was an automatic no. The thing is, we had church during the weekdays, which was also a no, so I didn't really have any other time to hang out with friends anyway. My parents didn't have a lot of extra money, so it was important that I help so my dad could possibly be done quicker to free up more time to get other jobs. The pastors even chipped in and took me to k-mart to get some clothes that were a little more age appropriate. Still not what I would have picked, and of course, all skirts and dresses, but they were way better than the granny clothes I had grown accustomed to wearing. Around this time as well, one of my dad's clients owned a dance studio so he would cut her grass for free in exchange for dance lessons. Finally! Something that a normal kid got to do!

I was in ballet and tap, but ballet was my favorite. I didn't have the grace of a ballerina but there was something about the movement and discipline that called to me. The class brought about a sense of peace and happiness I didn't really find anywhere else. Plus, who doesn't love a good tutu? I was given used tap and ballet shoes, but these hand-me-downs I cherished more than anything. I of course, wasn't allowed to be in the dance recital, partly because we couldn't afford the costumes but also because the church looked down on any form of dancing, so my mom was already breaking the rules for me to be able to participate in even the classes. I wish we hadn't gone to the recital because the moment she saw some of the dances of the older girls and the tight outfits, I wasn't allowed to go back. I was also working up the courage to ask if I could try out for the dance team at school, but given her reaction to the recital, I already knew that answer. I was crushed. My backup was the basketball team. No inappropriate costumes or gyrating of hips would for sure tarnish my soul and send me to hell...but practices and games fell on the days of church or work, so I wasn't allowed to do that either.

Now, I'm not a parent but my other peers had privileges. If they were bad or misbehaving, those privileges would be taken away. It was an incentive to do well in school, listen to your parents, etc. The thing is, I was never given incentives. No privileges. A reason to want to listen and not talk back. That was still my go-to tactic of mischief and mayhem. I didn't even have a TV in my room. At one point, I didn't have a door to my bedroom. I know those are typical teenage reprimands, but for me, it was just my life. At one point, I was missing so many days of school that an administrator called my mom to make sure everything was alright. Of course, she didn't tell them that if she left a bruise, welt, or mark on me that was visible, she would keep me from school. That spooked her because she had been to jail before, right around the time she had tried to adopt me and my sister, hence why she was ineligible. Did that stop the beatings though? No. She just got more careful not to leave marks. I still got in trouble at school. I think it was more of a cry for help because, again, I still wasn't able to deal with my emotions in a manner that wouldn't cause a disruption. I was drowning in my own pain and sadness, barely being let up to the surface to just breathe. Just be. I was written up multiple times. I received School Suspension, Out of School Suspension, and I even got the good ol' wooden paddle from the assistant principal. I felt like I was simply existing.

Going through the motions, just trying to get from one day to the next. I had a few friends in the neighborhood who went to the same school as me, and our moms would schedule times for us to hang out. The very few times they came to my house, I was always too embarrassed because of the way she'd yell at me in front of my friends or just loom over us, watching our every move and listening to our conversations. The hangouts became less and less frequent until they stopped altogether, and I didn't blame them. Plus, mothers didn't want their daughters hanging out with one of the school delinquents, which was entirely on me. I also ran away twice. My mom would call my friend's mothers in a frenzy. She wasn't close to them by any means but would feel the need to unburden herself, disclosing information that made them uncomfortable. Something needed to change. Clearly, it wasn't going to be my circumstances anytime soon, so it had to be me.

Chapter 14

I consider the 7th grade as my turning point. At 12 years of age, I decided that I couldn't be this version of myself anymore. My actions did have consequences that I, and I alone, caused. Yes, I had a rough childhood. Yes, my current life at home was challenging day in and day out. My only sense of relief was school, yet I was, in turn, making that hard and potentially jeopardizing the only escape I had from home by constantly getting into trouble. I had a lot of emotions. That fire within me was always ablaze, but my teachers, peers, and school staff weren't to blame. Yes, I was hurting. But the people I just mentioned weren't the cause. I needed to stop bleeding on everyone I encountered because I had open wounds that I didn't know how to heal. I needed to figure it out and make some changes. If I didn't, I would be what they thought of me. The lost cause. The bad seed. What was expected of me, given my past and current behavior, was to either end up in jail, on drugs or succumbing to an early grave.

I didn't want any of those outcomes for myself, so I simply needed to get out of my own way. People with troubled pasts tend to use the whole "You-don't-know-what-I've-been-through" phrase as a crutch. An excuse. Don't get me wrong, those feelings are 100% valid. I know firsthand how hard it is to keep the darkness at bay. No one knew what I had been through, nor did they know what I was going through. To say that none of them cared is a little dramatic, but in truth, they weren't overly concerned about my past but rather my present. Who I was in the moment. That was the test I was failing. I am naturally rebellious in the sense that I feel the need to question everything. I like to form opinions for myself, go against the grain, and have experiences through my lens, not that of someone else's. I wouldn't change that facet about myself for anything. But that didn't mean I had to challenge EVERYTHING, question EVERYTHING. I was a rebel without a cause, just being a menace for no other reason than I could. There was a time and a place for my rebellion, but I was even exhausting myself being so combative all the time. Another part of my lashing out at school was because my classmates would laugh and thought I was funny. With what I've endured, I relished in those moments because I felt like I belonged. I felt wanted. I felt valued. I went along with what the other kids were doing because I wanted to be accepted. During the 7th grade as well, we had a student transfer from another school. She was nice and pretty. One of the girls I hung out with decided one day that she didn't like her, so she wrote on a piece of paper, "I hate (Insert the new girl's name) and got most of our grade to sign it. The cool kids. The athletes. The cheerleaders. The entire paper was filled. I, in my misguided attempt to fit in, signed it as well. The paper was eventually given to the new girl during lunch when all of us were there, and we all witnessed her run out in tears. This was a classic case of bullying. Word on the street was my friend's crush stopped paying attention to her because he thought the new girl was cuter and wanted to get to know her instead. Typical mean girl behavior ensued. The thing is, I didn't like this version of myself that I was choosing to be in the hopes of social acceptance. I had been bullied my whole life. I knew exactly what that felt like. I decided then and there that I wasn't going to care what my peers thought of me because truth is, I still didn't get invited to parties or outings to the mall on the weekends. Well, partly because I'd always say no. I already knew what my mom was going to say anyway, so the invites stopped coming. My group of friends lived in the nicer neighborhoods and went shopping out of town, and took each other on their family vacations. I would always make up excuses as to why I wasn't doing those things, but it was because my family didn't have money like that. I simply was done. Done trying to be something I wasn't. I don't think I was fooling anyone anyway. And just like that, it was almost as if I was a different person overnight. I wasn't perfect by any means, but my behavioral issues substantially dipped. Something in my brain just clicked. I also needed to stop making excuses for myself. My past did hurt, but I was fully responsible for my present and future. Whew! What a year! I did a lot of personal growth and matured drastically in the 7th grade. I was gifted with self-awareness at a very young age, which was my saving grace. I needed to start taking some accountability because I was only making the situation worse for myself. I wanted to be better, and that is what I did.

8th grade came around, and I wanted to do things differently. I had always gotten good grades, so that wasn't the problem. This year, I wanted to try my hand at an extracurricular activity! I had to be careful about what I chose, making sure it was doable schedule wise, but also financially. I knew my parents didn't have a lot of extra money, so I had learned not to set myself up for disappointment by asking for things I knew we couldn't afford. I continued to sing, mostly in church, which made my mom proud. She never really said she was proud of me at this stage of my life, but I could see she took joy in having a talented daughter. When it came time for me to ask permission on which activity I chose, I chose something close to the vest, choir! It was a class offered in school, so it was free during school hours, and something I was already doing, singing. I was shocked when my mom said yes. The last year of middle school just got even better! Luckily, they had a used dress in my size because that was almost a deal breaker. Every excuse my mom tried to throw at me to say no, I had a rebuttal. A month or so into the school year, Show Choir tryouts were going to start, and I was determined to make the cut. My peers in the choir class said I probably wouldn't make it seeing as how this was my first year in choir, and I didn't know how to sight read yet. Little did they know, I had been singing almost my whole life, and I learned things quickly. I had this in the bag! And I did; I made the 8th Grade Show Choir! I was elated. I found my niche. I found the one thing to give my life meaning. Being part of the Show Choir meant you were a step above the rest, and I was determined to live up to my new expectations. We had extra performances we would do around town, which created a problem for my mom, seeing as how some of them landed on church days. She told me I would have to miss those performances or not be involved. I was starting to feel the sting of disappointment once again growing in the pit of my stomach. I went to school the next day, preparing myself to break the news to my choir teacher. I told her what my mom had said, and she said she would call her. She informed her that my participation was mandatory, only allowing me to miss 10% of the performances. She also talked about my potential and how much of an asset I would be and to let me have this opportunity. I guess hearing it from an adult was what my mom needed, and she allowed me to stay in the Show Choir. One of the biggest parts about being in the Show Choir was that we were now ambassadors of the school. This means our grades had to be above a certain GPA, and one referral or write up would be automatic expulsion. This was the final piece of the puzzle. I had something so precious to me that I would do anything to keep it. And I did just that. I had already started the process of growing out of my behavioral issues, but an opportunity such as this made it final. I was never a problem at school again.

Chapter 15

So, what exactly did I mean that my home life was a constant battle? To say my mom was controlling was an understatement. I only got my door back in high school. I didn't do anything to cause its removal; it was easier for her to keep an eye on my every move. I wasn't allowed a TV in my room, not because I was caught watching something I shouldn't, but to monitor what I did watch. I couldn't watch Harry Potter because witchcraft was of the devil. Disney Channel was even banned because they would play "secular" music videos in between the shows...Disney kid music videos. My favorite show, The Golden Girls, was the worst of all which made me sad. I mean, I didn't quite blame her for that one because of Blanche, but still.My only options were to watch sports with my dad or novellas with my mom, and that's why I'm such a sports fan. And some of these novellas could put Balance Deveraux to shame, but when I brought that up, it just ended in an argument. As I entered my formative years, things only got worse. High school came around, and the leash only got tighter. I wanted to play sports, but of course, those were shot down to focus on my academics because college was around the corner. I didn't fight that though, if I could still be in choir, which was allowed. I honestly wanted to fill my calendar with as many activities, so I didn't have to be home as much.

We came to an agreement that I could wear pants on Tuesdays and Thursdays while still having to wear a dress or skirt on Mondays, Wednesdays, and Fridays. This wasn't ideal, but I went along with this too. I was slowly learning not to make mountains out of molehills, as they say in the south. I had to let the little things go to prevent arguments. No one will ever know just how much I bit my tongue because everything was a debate, an argument, a sin. Now, I will admit that at times, I couldn't control my mouth, and I paid the price dearly. I believe that children need to be reprimanded. I'll even go to say that I deserved a slap in the face from time to time. But getting backhanded to the face is abuse. Getting hair pulled out and blood drawn is abuse. Getting slammed against walls and choked is abuse. I once had a knife held to my cheek, all because I didn't instantly get up and do the dishes. I wanted to finish my homework first. Having to explain that cut on my face was so much fun at school. Wooden spoons became extinct in my house. Having to act normal and put on a smile after those incidents on our way to praise God at church was particularly amusing to me. That smirk I would have on my face because of the irony definitely got me smacked and punched on the ride there. I was getting older, though, and the abuse had lost its power over me if it had any to begin with. I would just sit and take it. I wouldn't give a reaction. I wouldn't even flinch. I wouldn't cower. At times, I would smile just to upset her, and suddenly, I was possessed by a demon. I was told that a lot. In my naivete, I tried to pray the demon away, thinking that maybe there was something incredibly wrong with me. Why did I constantly attract the darkness? Not only within myself but within others as well? Why was I the magnet for chaos, even when I wasn't the one causing it? Remember when I said that I had a knack for bullying my bullies right back? But what happens when your biggest bully is your own mother?

When I hit puberty, I gained a lot of weight and would end up being at my heaviest. My mom was a good cook; what can I say? But also, sports were always out of the question to keep me active. Music was becoming a big part of my life. So much so that I decided at a very young age that was what I wanted to pursue when I got older. Around the age of 15, my mom had a cute idea for me to record a Christmas CD instead of your typical holiday greeting card. We went to a local recording studio where I sang two Christmas songs and a Christian one. I will say that she always supported my singing...as long as it was for God. The man who recorded me told my mom that I had promise. I was very talented at such a young age, and if I continued to work on my craft, he could really see me making it big time. Oh, but I would need to lose weight, of course. She was elated to hear this and told him she would work on me losing weight. I don't know if this conversation was supposed to be between them two, but I heard every word and instantly felt inadequate. What a shame; everything was going so well. My mom proudly handed out the CDs to everyone who would take them, including the church folk, friends, and family. She wasn't lying about doing her part to make me skinny. Locks went on the fridge and pantry for a time. She was already hard on me to always look presentable when we left the house. Hair done. Makeup on. Respectable outfit. But in the way she wanted, which ended in plenty of arguments. I always loved makeup and fashion, but I could never express it in the ways that I wanted to because I'd end up in Hell.

I did get put on discipline at church once for wearing clear mascara. Oh, the calamity! What a scandal, I tell you! Good times. Adding my caloric intake made her unbearable. She had a comment every time a fork went to my mouth. Should I be eating that? Haven't I had enough? Did I want to stay fat for the rest of my life? According to her, no man would ever love me, and I wouldn't be successful in music if I ate too much. I was too pretty to be fat...if I had a dollar for every time I heard that phrase in my life, I could have fronted my entire music career! The thing is my mom had very little tact when it came to her criticism. What embarrassed me the most was when she would say these things in front of company, whether we were at a restaurant or eating at someone's house. She wasn't nice about it either. Sometimes, it was so disruptive to the dinner table, and people would be sitting there awkwardly or trying to change the subject as quickly as possible. The irony was that my mom was overweight and had been most of her life. Also, in our household, we didn't waste food, so I was forced to eat everything that was put on my plate. If I didn't, I'd be accused of being ungrateful or anorexic, which wasn't the case at all. This was a battle I couldn't win. No matter what I did, it wasn't right. Even my dad's nickname for me was Gorda or Gordita (fat girl). As one can imagine, this did wonders for a teenage girl's self-esteem. It's always the parent's fault, right? But if the shoe fits...

In my fight for normalcy, I wanted to hang out with a friend. I made sure all my chores were done my homework completed, and I even helped my dad with the yardwork so there wasn't an excuse to say no. So, the moment of truth came. It was time for me to ask. I gave her all the details: where I was going, who I was going with, who all was going to be there, etc. To my surprise, she said yes if I had finished all my chores and homework. Ha! I was three steps ahead of her there! To her even bigger surprise, she started her inspection. The laundry was completed and folded away. Dishes were done. My bathroom was spotless. Everything was in its place in my room and closets. I wasn't allowed closet doors either to make sure they were always clean anyway. Not a speck of dust was to be found. Time to check under the bed. Crap! Didn't think to check there. One singular red shirt that I hadn't noticed had fallen from my laundry basket and was on the floor right by my bed skirt. Because of this, my mom recanted her "yes" with a big fat "no."

I was beside myself. I had been looking forward to escaping my house for just a short while and actually having some fun. She walked out, and if I could have slammed my door, I would have, but I was to have the door always open, even when I slept. The only exception was when I was changing, and trust me, if I took too long doing that, the door would be opened unannounced. The lock had been tampered with, so I wasn't able to lock my door even if I tried. I was trying so hard to collect myself and keep a cool head, but I was fuming. I picked the shirt up and threw it at my open door at the same time my mom had returned to hear what I was mumbling under my breath...and it hit her right in the face. Now to be honest, it was a hilarious moment. The timing couldn't have been more perfect. In a family sitcom, this would have been when the audience would erupt with uncontrollable laughter. We both stood there stunned for a moment, but I started to back up for fear of what was coming next. She lunged toward me, knocking me onto my bed, and grabbed me by my hair, and started punching me in my head and face. She had pulled me off my bed by my hair, which as one could imagine, really hurt, so I dug my nails as hard as I could into her arm. This didn't stop her, so I used all my strength to push her off me. She fell back into my doorless closet, shocked. The thing is, I was 5'8' and naturally muscular. As my parents put it, I was "built for manual labor." My mom was maybe 5'1' and heavier set, but she didn't stand a chance against me. This was the first time I fought back. The first time, I stood up for myself. At 16 years of age, I had had enough. I snapped and shoved her off me for once. Now, of course, that wasn't the story that was told. Here I was being deemed a danger to others again. I was abusing my mother. I was starting to throw things at her face that could cause her harm. I had left marks on her arm from where I had dug my nails, and she wore that as evidence of my mistreatment. Excuse me for not having the foresight to leave marks where no one could see like she did. I didn't care, though. I never felt the need to prove or stand up for myself to her friends, church people, or her family. What I had been through thus far in my life made me not care if I was painted the villain or not. I knew the truth, and that is all that mattered to me.

Due to the event mentioned above, my mom decided it was time for some family counseling. In her eyes, things had gotten out of control, and she no longer felt safe around me, which was laughable. I was defending myself. She was hurting me, and I did what I could to have it stop. But I went along with it. If a counselor could truly help us, it would be worth a shot. She insisted on having joint sessions, which Is how I guess family counseling worked. We only went to one session. The counselor commended me for being a functioning member of society, telling me that most children with my background aren't as well adjusted as I was. A functioning member of society...That was the first time I remembered an adult acknowledging that I had come so far, and she didn't even know me personally. It was reassuring because no one truly knew just how hard I had worked to be a different person, no, a different child. After all, even at this moment, I was still a child. It was so tiring at times because those memories were forever present, looming in the back of my mind, and the demons they created relentlessly clawing away at my sanity, my soul. I had stopped making excuses for my bad behavior a long time ago, but if I were going to be honest, I had legitimate "excuses," especially as a child. Adults, since practically birth, had written me off as a lost cause. I was simply too damaged and beyond broken to be worth any form of consideration, love, tenderness, or even care. Why was that so hard of a concept for the adults in my life to understand that? I was still the victim here, not the villain...a victim! To this day, I still use that term, that phrase, to categorize my triumph. I am a functioning member of society dammit! Our first session did not go over well with my mom. I think the counselor validating my traumas was the first thing to go wrong in her eyes. How dare she take my side, which wasn't what she did; she just tried to point out that I wasn't entirely to blame for our familial issues. Every time the counselor asked me a question, my mom would answer for me and not let me speak. I would let her finish her complaints and concerns but was never allowed a rebuttal. I was instantly verbally attacked, being blamed for all our issues and even so much as bringing up my childhood as some sort of proof that

me in front of my closest friends or in front of church people like that was normal behavior. It was all starting to wear me down. My behavior was noticeably different at school. Teachers started to express their concerns. I would always say I was fine, just tired. DCF (Department of Children and Families) got called quite a few times, and the case workers would come to talk to me at school, and I could always convince them that I was ok and that nothing was wrong. The last time though, in my junior year of high school, I practically begged them not to get my mom involved. I guess I wasn't convincing this time, and they made a home visit. That landed me in very hot water, as one could imagine. Instead of possibly seeing that as a cry for help, I found myself getting "disciplined" even more, which didn't help our situation. The figurative noose around my neck was tighter than ever.

Fast forward to the Fall of my Senior year of high school. I was excited like most of my peers but for different reasons. Yes, I was looking forward to the freedom that came with going to college and being on my own, but for me, I was looking forward to peace, being able to just breathe. Naturally, that wasn't what my mom wanted. She wanted me to still live at home and attend the local community college. I was absolutely against that for obvious reasons. I couldn't stay in this house anymore. Most of my friends were a year older than me and had already moved on. The few that I had left were also going to major universities hours away. I was going to be alone, with no escape from my home life. I wasn't allowed my own computer and when my mom wasn't home, the wifi box was locked in her room. She even went to school to try to limit my access to the internet without supervision, which they couldn't promise. We had protective blocks at school, but what she wanted to prevent me from doing was applying to colleges. When I had to use the internet at home, she would be looming over my shoulder or have me do whatever I needed to do in the same room as she was, with the screen facing her. For one of my classes, I had to do a research project which needed me to be on the internet longer than usual. My mom wasn't happy, but she obliged because this was a big part of my grade for this class. She was constantly yelling at me to hurry up, asking me what was taking so long, and even standing over my shoulder for a time. I was in the same room as my parents, who were watching tv. I wasn't doing anything I wasn't meant to do; it was just taking time. She finally got fed up with how long I was on the computer and got up to turn the laptop to her. When she did this, the computer fell to the floor, which made her furious. I was so anxious and heated that I got up to get something to eat and take a break. I had peeped my head into the fridge to look to see what was at the bottom when my mom took the fridge door and slammed it into my head, which hurt a lot. I started to yell back at her, asking her why she did this and that to forget it; I didn't care if I finished my paper at this point or got a bad grade in the class. I was just fed up. I went to my room and slammed the door, and started crying. I didn't realize that I had slammed it so hard that my unlockable door locked for the first time since living in that house. Remember, my dad had finagled it so I wouldn't be able to lock my door, ever. Of course, this upset my mom, and she demanded I open the door and keep it open like I was supposed to. I refused because I was so upset. I don't know what led my parents to do this, but they decided to take hammers to my door. I also don't know what led me to put my back against the door they were taking hammers to, but all I knew was that I didn't want them coming in. So, there they were, tearing down my door to the point where they were now hitting my back with their hammers. They finally stopped when they achieved their goal. I was distraught. My head was still throbbing with having a fridge door slammed against it, and now I felt the sting of fresh wounds on my back. I'm not proud of what I did next, but I believe I suffered some sort of mental breakdown.

I searched my room for scissors, a wire hanger, anything sharp enough because I had every intention of taking my life that day. I couldn't find anything sharp enough, so I rammed my fist against my window in the hopes that I would shatter the glass to use the shards. I was too big to fit through it because I would have run away and never returned. I tried a few more times to break my window but was unsuccessful. In the movies, they make it look so simple. I didn't have pills in my room either, so my last resort was to ram my head against the wall, which I did, but that hurt too much, so I just slid to the floor, crying in disbelief. In my frenzy of trying to find something to end my life, I saw that I had a disposable camera and decided to take pictures of my door and my back.

I didn't sleep at all that night, also because my parents would peep through the open cracks of my door to make sure

I was still there or alive. I was also upset because I didn't know what to tell my teacher as to why I didn't finish my final assignment for the class. I was forced to go to work with my mom the next day to finish my paper, under her supervision, of course. I couldn't concentrate, which made her mad, so I just sat there, a zombie. I went to school the following day, a complete emotional mess. I tried my hardest to keep myself together, but I broke down the moment I saw my teacher. I asked for more time, which she allowed.

I hadn't gone into detail, but she knew that it must have been something bad for me to act this way. I was usually very composed, no matter what. But my spirit had been broken once again. My closest friend at the time knew something was incredibly wrong, and after a few tries, I told her what happened. She knew of my situation all too well, seeing my mom in action many times. Her mom and my mom also had a history, and it actually took her a while to even warm up to me. She told me that I was not going back to my home, that it was no longer safe for me. I didn't have the mental strength to put up a fight, and quite frankly, I didn't want to anyway. My friend's mom called my house to inform my mom that I wouldn't be returning home. Later that night, we stopped by to pick up some of my belongings, but there were several trash bags already set out in the yard. My friend let me stay at her house for the remainder of my senior year since her brother was away at college. Staying under the same roof as my best friend was a change I welcomed whole-heartedly. Maybe I could have the normal senior year I longed for after all.

Chapter 17

While the best friend I had at the time and I have since grown apart, she and her family were a godsend. I will not go too much into her story because it is Her's to tell, but we had a lot in common, especially our childhoods. She too was adopted and more or less understood what I was going through. I never felt judged by her because in truth, she had no right to judge. Her adoption was a different story, being adopted by liberal parents with money. I only bring this up because, from the beginning, they welcomed me in as their own. This ordeal with me leaving home happened right around the holidays, and I had family dinners with them and spent Christmas with them as part of their family. I had a job after school, and while my friend had a car, she would sometimes be working, and one of her parents never hesitated to take me to work or pick me up. I also was alleviated by the burden of spending so much time at church. Remember, I was forced to spend 4-5 nights there. What to do with all this freedom? Well, I spent It with my best friend, of course. She lived on the lake with a pool, and her parents would often go out of town, which meant throwing parties! I have fond memories of doing her hair and makeup and picking out her outfits. Although I was never really allowed to show it, I have always been the fashionista of the group.

I had missed the deadline to apply to the colleges I really wanted to go to or got denied because I was a late applicant and most colleges had already accepted the quota of the up-and-coming freshman class. It was my dream to attend Florida State University with my best friend and be suitemates, go to parties, and navigate the sea that would have been college boys. I only applied to a handful of colleges because I was running out of time now that it was the spring semester of my senior year. All that work to make good grades and take AP classes seemed silly now. I got accepted into the University of Central Florida, but only if I could start in the summer, which was just a few months away. Plus, it was a little too close to home. I also got accepted into a college in Tampa, but it was a private school with private school prices. I finally chose to go to the University of West Florida, admittedly only because the website depicted it as on the beach which I always loved. Because my mom was adamant about me staying home, I missed out on college tours and learning about financial aid and my other options. I was learning these things on the fly, and it was all very overwhelming to me. It was not fun at all trying to do all these things at the last minute. It was also a sad time because this process was supposed to be a time of joy and great anticipation for the future.

I was able to attend a lot of the senior events now and even attended my first prom, my senior prom. I wasn't allowed to go to homecomings or proms because secular music was played, and often, drinking could be involved. Oh, and the dresses that were worn were way too revealing, my mom's words, not mine. I was forced to miss out on so much, all in the name of God and my mom's tyranny. My parents showed up to my senior winter concert, which fell on a church day, so I was surprised. My concerts seemed to always be on church days, so my parents never went to them. Because you know, it's a cardinal sin to miss a day of church to go to your daughter's school event, knowing it would have meant the world to her to have her parents in the crowd. The one time they did, was ruined by the last memory of them, taking hammers to my door and my back. I had my senior solo to sing. It was our winter concert, so I chose "A Christmas Song." With the lights blinding me, I hadn't noticed their presence. I sang my heart out, trying not to cry because I only had a few chances left to do this before I graduated. The thunderous applause and the standing ovation I received is some of the greatest moments of my life to this day. It is also the reason I will always choose opportunities to sing, no matter where life takes me. On stage, I'm not my pain. I'm not my circumstances. I can forget, even for the briefest of moments. I could hide behind a performance, disguising my tears as just being overcome by the music, giving it my all, and not holding back like you're supposed to. My peers never knew what pain I was masking, hiding behind my jokes and great performances. I had gotten good at hiding abuse. When the concert was over, that's when I saw them because they were coming towards me. My mom had a talent for pretending like nothing was wrong, talking to the other parents about how talented I was, and chiming in on their praises, which was news to me. According to her, I would never amount to anything if my singing wasn't going to be for God. They tried to make conversation with me and even gave me flowers, and I remember thinking that it was the first time I had seen my dad cry. I didn't reciprocate, but I was cordial enough. I planned to never speak to them again. I was off to college soon and wouldn't look back at my small town and the memories it held there, but I was running out of options towards the summer. My best friend's brother was coming back for summer break so I couldn't stay there. I crashed with another friend and her family for the summer, but I was beginning to be too much for them since they lived in a much smaller house. I was sleeping in the same room as my other close friend, and I started to feel unwelcome. She had two other siblings, while I grew up as an only child. I clearly had taken for granted having my own room and bathroom. A bigger family meant budget-friendly meals, which wasn't what I was accustomed to either. My mom was a great cook and enjoyed making meals for myself and my dad. We also sat at the table every night as a family, even when my teenage self didn't want to. Unfortunately, I showed my disapproval on my face, which was heartbreaking to hear. My face and my brain struggle to get on the same page occasionally. That was the beginning of the end of our friendship, and I take full responsibility for not invalidating anyone's feelings even though, in my mind, I was being completely misunderstood.

My best friend's parents treated me like an extension of their family, buying me Christmas presents and inviting me to a few of their vacations. One day, my best friend's mom, as she was taking me to work, said something to me that shook me to my core, "You know, a thank you every once in a while goes a long way." I was taken aback because I was so unbelievably grateful. Who knows what would have happened if it wasn't for their charity, taking me in when they did. One of two things would have happened: I would have run away, and who knows what would have happened to me, or I would have made sure I was more prepared the next time I wanted to take my life. I apologized repeatedly and poured out my thanks. Since then, I have tried to say thank you for even the smallest of acts or charity. In truth, I was attempting to hide my embarrassment by masking it as pride. I didn't want to come off as the poor friend, even though that is what I was. My best friend or her parents never made me feel that way, ever. I started to feel my sheltered life seeping through. I was thankful to learn a few of these lessons, even though those growing pains hurt immensely. It was a further reminder that while my mom had her faults, I too had mine. I think the universe wanted me to not forget that. It is so easy to form a victim-complex, especially when circumstances in one's life tend to have an ongoing theme of heartbreak, disappointment, and abuse.

My heart started to soften a bit, realizing that the main reason my mom and I never really got along was because we were very similar. We both were strong-will, stubborn women who liked to be in control. The time came for me to go to college, and I honestly was forced to reach back out to my parents because I didn't have any help moving. They had tried to reach me, but again, I was too immature at the time to accept their apology. They practically tried to buy my forgiveness by getting me some much-needed dorm essentials and school supplies. I didn't mind because doing everything on my own was stressing me out. I worked part-time at Panera Bread, so I did the best I could, but it wasn't nearly enough. I was also reminded that while we didn't have much, my parents always tried their best. I never held that against them. Don't get me wrong, I am a brat, but I am so grateful that I wasn't THAT type of brat. I was given the typical sendoff, getting reminded that I was a woman of the Lord, so not participating in drinking or drug-use was a must if I wanted to enter the gates of heaven. My mom had found the vibrator my friends had gotten me for one of my birthdays when she went through my things when I moved out and took the opportunity to remind me that those types of feelings were meant to be shared with my future husband and only my future husband. I know she was worried because I was leaving the nest for good, but I reminded her as well that she needed to trust her parenting. Despite everything, I was a decent human being and a woman with a good head on her shoulders. I was going to make mistakes, but that wouldn't reflect on her. I was and have always been my own person. She should have known that better than anyone for all the times she tried to break that person. We got to the college, and I had to take whatever dorm was left because I didn't realize that was something you were supposed to do ahead of time as well as get to know your roommate. Again, I was doing all this at the last minute. She gave me pointers on how I should decorate my very small side of the dorm and scoffed at what very little closet space I had. She was trying; I couldn't deny that. My parents gave me their farewell hugs, with my mom failing very badly at trying to hold back her tears. She very rarely gave me a compliment or said she was proud of me. I'm not sure why it was so damn hard for her to say those words out loud, but in that moment, I knew she was proud. And I could live with that. I had grown accustomed to just accepting what she could never say to me.

Things eventually got back to normal with me and my parents. Our relationship did seem to be better when there was some distance between us. I had no choice but to go home for college breaks because I had felt like I overstayed my welcome in my friend's houses. Enough time had passed where at least the sting of the incident wasn't fresh on our minds. We never really seemed to talk things out. We would simply let enough time pass. It would mostly end up in an argument, so it was never worth it to me to stand up for myself and explain my side. I was making friends, and they were honestly my lifeline. They started to notice a pattern, though. When I went home for so much as a holiday, I would figuratively fall off the face of the earth. A slight depression would kick in because I hated being home. Something about my hometown and being within close proximity to my mom just drained me. It was so much work, mentally and emotionally, to brave the storm that was always us two in the same room. I put the blame on myself as well because there were times when I couldn't keep my mouth shut, and I would argue back. I was by no means perfect either. I know I did things in my youth to cause her grief. There was also the elephant in the room, forever present, forever growing, and that was her physical and emotional abuse. I did my best to ignore it, but it also took even more mental strength to sit across the room, side by side at church, sit amongst her friends, and pretend like we were this loving mother/daughter duo. Add to the mix that there was simply nothing to do in my hometown and you had the perfect recipe for me turning into a zombie. I admit that the trips home became less frequent. I valued my freedom. I valued my peace of mind. I valued being able to discover who I truly was without constant ridicule, without being told that breathing the wrong way would put me in defiance of God and send me to hell without the constant tension. That tension, I know, was one of the reasons she became sickly around this time. She had always had health issues on and off, but when I was in college, that is when the slow decline started to happen. My mom was...intense...with everyone. She meant well, but I genuinely believe that was why she was in and out of hospitals to the point where she couldn't work a normal job, which took a toll on my dad as he was now the main provider of the household. Around my sophomore year of college, despite our turbulent relationship, I was debating moving to a college closer to home to help my dad with the doctor's appointments and probably even financially. I was saddened at the thought because I loved the life I had built in Pensacola, Fl. My friends my coworkers, they were becoming like my family, and it was going to be hard to leave them. "You're pretty, and people naturally like you, so you'll do just fine. I was never like that." my mom said. I looked at her, completely shocked. It was a rarity for her to give me a compliment, let alone tell me I was pretty. That was the first time that I could remember her flat out just saying it without a follow-up or a "but" with a negative comment about my weight or my hair that usually followed. She was always so hard on my appearance. Hair always had to be done. Clothes and makeup needed always to be presentable but not too worldly or I was going to hell. I ate too much. I was too lazy, and that's why I was fat. And according to her, I was the spawn of Satan, the bad seed that would never amount to anything. I wasn't aware that in her eyes, I would have enough redeemable qualities for people to "naturally like me," you know, for being the spawn of Satan and all. At that moment, her constant ridicule made a little more sense to me, and all I felt was pity. She pulled through that health scare, so there was no need for me to transfer schools, and for that, I was grateful. That particular summer was a hard one. The thought of returning home brought the seasonal depression early. My friends started throwing farewell parties and get-togethers, which tore me apart even more. I had missed so many of my summer classes while going back home that I failed them all which plummeted my GPA one whole point. It never did recover after that. What made matters worse was that I was slated to hold a leadership position in my sorority in the upcoming fall semester as well as be an Orientation Leader, something I had wanted to do since my own freshman orientation, and I lost both positions due to my GPA no longer meeting the requirements. I appealed to have those grades removed from my record to at least salvage my GPA as best as I could, and that too was denied. I even brought in my mom's hospital paperwork, and she had went as far as to write a letter disclosing her health issues and hospital stay, how she was on life support, and that is why I had missed so many of my classes. Her plea didn't make a difference, but I appreciated her trying. I learned a valuable lesson that summer. And that was that no matter what justifications I thought I had in life to excuse my actions, they would always have consequences, no matter what. The world didn't care. Life keeps progressing forward; it doesn't stop for anyone or anything. That was a harsh reality I have learned over and over.

Chapter 18

Fast forward a little bit to when I graduated college. It wasn't a memorable occasion for me because my two best friends at the time couldn't make it even though I made it to both of theirs. I had even taken a greyhound bus for 5 hours since my car had recently broken down because I knew just how important it was to be there. None of my coworkers, who were also some of my closest friends, could make it because someone had to work, which made sense, but still, I was let down. My parents drove the 8ish hours to Pensacola because my intentions were to move back home for a bit to save money, so I needed help transporting all my belongings. That, of course, was a big ask, even though I reminded my mom that I was graduating, so weren't they planning on coming up anyway? No response. When my parents got there, my mom started complaining. The car ride was too long. They were going to be spending money they didn't have on gas. It was too hot. Why did I have so many things they needed to put in the car? I was already upset that none of my friends were going to make it, and as one could imagine, she wasn't doing anything to make the situation better. The morning of my graduation, all she did was complain about having to climb the stadium stairs. Why was it going to be outside? It was going to be too hot. Why was the ceremony going to last that long? Now, they'd get home too late. We wouldn't have money for a nice dinner to celebrate because they'd spent it on the trip up there. I finally snapped and told her we could skip the ceremony since it would be too much for her to see her daughter graduate college. I reminded her that she too, had missed my high school graduation. I wasn't keeping track or anything...I was beside myself. My big day was ruined. I had spent money on a cap and gown and bought my sashes and pins, all for nothing. Usually, this was such a joyous occasion for families. It is a big deal for someone to graduate college. I just wanted this one day to be about me. I finally snapped and yelled for us to forget it and just go home. I did make sure she knew how I felt; that she had ruined my day, which naturally ended with us having a big argument. Of course, that was my fault. Everything was always my fault. I sat in silence the entire car ride home, not looking forward to being under the same roof as my mom again and in my small town.

With college now over with, I put a lot of my efforts into how I could move to California. I still had every intention of pursuing music and always wanted to live in a flashy city like Los Angeles. I had gotten my first "big girl" job but still chose to live at home to save money for my relocation to the west coast. Big mistake. I admit I had California on my mind and talked about it every second I could with anyone who would listen. My mom, one morning grew tired of my banter, telling me that I was never going to make it out in California and that my music career would never happen if it wasn't going to be all for God. With what money? Without family or friends? Without her? I would fall flat on my face, and she couldn't wait for that reality check to hit me. I told her I disagreed, saying that I was capable of more things than she thought and that I wanted to get as far away from her as I could. Admittingly, I shouldn't have said that, but in the same breath of admittance, I meant it with every fiber of my being. My mom's old instinctual reaction came bubbling to the surface, and she slapped me across my face as hard as she could. We both stood there for a second in utter shock and silence. I had my lunch box in my hand because I was waiting for my dad to take me to work, and in a brief swoop, I hit her across the face with it and told her that I wasn't a little girl anymore. I was a grown woman of 23 years of age. She was not going to use me as her punching bag, and if she did that again, she was going to regret it. Now, I won't lie, that felt good. To see the shock on her face, her hand on her cheek, her eyes filled with rage yet holding back tears. It felt good to stand up for myself, for real this time finally. If it wasn't for my dad stepping in when he did and pushing me out the door, I probably would have hit her again. I had years of anger and animosity towards her right below the surface of my skin, waiting to erupt like a volcano. Bring it! I was ready. I was also ready to accept whatever consequences my actions would have brought. Now, before I get judged too harshly, it was a cloth lunch bag, and I only had a sandwich and a bag of chips in there ok!

The only hurt I caused was probably to her ego. I started looking for apartments the moment I got to work and moved out by the end of the month. I was saving up for a car and California anyway, so I had the money for moving expenses. Again, there wasn't a conversation, just time that passed by before we were at least on speaking terms. I don't quite remember how this happened, but around this time, my sister and I had found one another again and were on speaking terms. One thing led to another, and she ended up moving to Florida and living with me for a time. After almost 20 years, we were reunited.

You had never met two siblings that were opposites like we were. She was short. I was tall. She liked video games. I liked sports. She was a tom boy. I was girly. She was messy. I was a neat freak. She was super religious. The only thing I did religiously was take my birth control. She was passive-aggressive. I was highly assertive (ok fine, sometimes aggressive too). She was a hugger. I tensed up at any form of affection, so yea, let's keep the hugging to a minimum. She was warm and inviting. I was emotionally distant and reserved. I could see why she was the favorite growing up. Getting to know each other all over again proved difficult at times because we couldn't be more different, but we were the only family we had, so we did the best we could. I will admit that even to this day, we aren't as close as I would have wished, and I take full responsibility for that. Having a legitimate family, being a big sister, was a part I wasn't prepared to play. In truth, that part of my heart was closed off as well. We began sharing our stories of our upbringing. She was misinformed on a lot of details pertaining to me. That's not a shocker. She also wasn't aware of all I had endured in my childhood either. I grew up being so envious of her because she had a family and parents who loved her. Big birthday parties and happy Christmases, but what was shocking to me was that she too, had suffered with our adoptive parents. I'll leave it at that because again, that is her story to tell. The one thing our childhoods had in common was physical abuse, which breaks my heart to even write. The Lajas's were never physically or emotionally abusive towards me, but she had been there longer and suffered much as well. My mom was ecstatic, as one could imagine. She finally had both her girls back, the blessing she had prayed for for decades. Her prayers were inevitably answered, probably not in the timeline she had thought, but better late than never, I guess. We got paraded at church again as the miracle, and maybe there was some truth to her proclaimations this time. It was nothing short of a miracle that we ended up together and back with one of our foster families we knew as toddlers no less. That just doesn't happen, but here we were. I was naturally protective of her when it came to my mom because I knew how quick my mom was to want to control the things around her. My sister was more passive and possibly wouldn't stand up for herself like I did. As good as I was at setting boundaries with my mom, at times, I even gave in to not having to feel her wrath or being in a constant state of combativeness. I was so over the constant. state. of. combativeness. I know I played a part in that state as well, so that's why I'd cave into her wishes or just not be present around her. Can't control what isn't there you feel me? I also knew what my sister had already been through, and I was dammed if she had to suffer even more, not on my watch! She already had enough wounds to heal. Oh, how I wish someone had shielded me. Given me some time to let my wounds heal before fresh ones were thrashed upon me. Maybe my wounds wouldn't be so deep...My sister got along with my mom surprisingly well. My dad, not so much. Not that they didn't get along, but they really didn't have a lot in common. I was the one that was closest to my dad, which we kept being told was the opposite when we were with them as young children. I was skeptical because I could never imagine a time when me and my mom were thick as thieves, as she would put it. Not with what we've been through up to this point. My sister was aware of the abuse committed by my mom. I even showed her the pictures of my back and the door from high school. I just wish I had thought to take more pictures of all the countless other instances. But she believed me, despite my mom telling her she never laid a hand on me when she was asked about it. I didn't even know what to say. That was a blatant lie, but I didn't have the energy to confront my mom about it. I did ask her once about my "red memory," the one I talked about at the beginning. The one with me covered in my own blood, with it all over my sheets and walls. She was the one who told me I was being "disciplined" with her hands beating me to that point and not letting up, even though I was pleading, and getting hit even more for it. That memory still keeps me up at night at times. I let it go, not caring enough to ask about her sheer delusion. Fine, I gave myself all those bruises and pulled out my own hair. I would throw myself against walls and make my own nose bleed countless times. Ok, fine.

On December 14th, 2014, I had a life-altering experience in the form of being diagnosed with an auto immune disease. That is a different story for another time, but in this moment, I wanted my life to be different. California was put back on the table, and it looked like it was going to work out for me this time. If I was annoying about it before, I was insufferable now because it was actually happening. My relocation to the west coast was finally happening! Even though we lived in the same town and almost in the same neighborhood, my mom pointed out that she felt like she saw me less than when I was away at college. There was a reason for this, but maybe she never truly realized it. I told her I never came over because all we do is fight, to which she responded with, "At least that's something." Not for me mom, not for me. That toxic environment had affected us both mentally and now physically. She was now on dialysis three times a week while I was still reeling from my recent diagnosis. I literally couldn't afford the stress on my body anymore. But at that moment, I obliged, knowing that I was due to be thousands of miles away in a few months, so we had very little time. I of course, talked about my move to California. She frustratingly told me that I was never going to get to where I wanted to until I just accepted that I was from a small town and a poor family. Those words struck a chord in me, and I wouldn't truly understand them until I was submerged in the new city that was Los Angeles. But again, another story for another time. She had called me once at work, missing me and wanting to know what I was up to. I could tell she was feeling the distance between us, and I hadn't even left yet. I was completely honest and told her I was looking up the neighborhood I was moving to and attempting to familiarize myself with the streets and locating where all my basic necessities were like the grocery stores, gym, etc. On company time, of course. This upset her, and she started going in on me again. How I was going to fall flat on my face. How she was only going to give me 3 months out there on my own before I came crawling back home. How music wasn't going to happen for me because I had chosen to write secular music and not music for God. Luckily, I had my own office at the time because I snapped. I told her, "You know, I rarely doubt myself, but on the rare occasions that I do, it's your voice in my head that is screaming at me, telling me how I'll never amount to anything. That I am, in fact, too damaged to ever be normal, to ever be loved. When I can't even stand to look at my own reflection in the mirror, it is your voice in my head, screaming at me at how fat and ugly I am. How no man will ever love the lazy piece of shit that I am. Do you think that is normal? Are you really going to sit there and act like you don't have the slightest clue as to why I want to move clear across the country? It's to get away from you. And trust me, 3000 miles doesn't seem far enough." She stayed on the phone for a few seconds in silence, not knowing what to say. When she finally said something, she couldn't understand why I would feel that way and told me I was being unfair. I didn't have any more fight left in me, and if she couldn't possibly understand the words that just came out of my mouth, then nothing else could be said. I sat and sobbed in my office. It was the type of sob that purged the soul. I hadn't realized just how much I was holding back. I had always tried to paint myself as someone who doesn't feel, who doesn't care enough to be bothered. But truth be told, I am the opposite. I feel too deeply; I just have an unhealthy habit of suppressing my emotions. It was the first time I had said that out loud. I had finally given the voices in my head a name, and that name was my mother. That revelation made me incredibly sad. I wasn't well versed in what healthy mother-daughter relationships looked like, but I knew it wasn't this. I had yet again, unknowingly ripped off the band aid. But what was it that Taylor Swift said? "Band-Aids don't fix bullet holes." These wounds were just too deep. I needed to put distance between us permanently if we wanted to even be on speaking terms. My mind was ready to leave and never look back, but my heart was still holding on to the chance that one day, maybe one day, things could be different between us. Even as I get older, that little girl who just wanted a family that loved her is within me somewhere, still clinging to a glimmer of hope.

Before I left for California, I had a few doctor's appointments to check off my list. One was about an hour and a half away, and my mom insisted on taking me. I obliged, knowing that it would mean a lot to her. I felt ok, but she still wanted to hear what the doctor had to say. We only had a few more chances like this, anyway. On the way there, I felt the need to apologize, not for my recent comments or moving across the country, but for being so closed off from the beginning. I expressed that when I came to live with her at the age of 11, I was already too far gone. I had already known such heartbreak and disappointment, so I chose to close off my heart. I had given up on what it could truly mean to have a family. I know I wasn't the loving daughter she had hoped for, and I admitted the part I felt I played in why we never grew close. Seeing how naturally warm and loving my sister was, and having my best friend causally comment how it took me months, or even over a year, for me to tell her I loved her and accept her hugs, and repeatedly hearing from men trying to date me that I didn't open up, I realized that I had built my walls up so high and that even those who did care for me still felt at arm's length. I had made my armor impenetrable, often coming off as cold-hearted and distant. Blame it on my reactive attachment disorder or my unwillingness to be vulnerable. Hell, blame it on being an Aquarius; my point was that I was acknowledging at that moment that I shared blame for our issues. I also admitted that we were too much alike, adding to the constant arguments and tension (again, admitting blame). I called her out on her obsessive need to be in control, especially when it came to me, and that was one of the biggest factors that pushed me away.

I needed to truly find myself, find my own voice, find my way to loving who I was unconditionally, and I couldn't do that with her constant ridicule. Her voice was the loudest in my head most times, and I wished that what I heard were words of kindness, encouragement, and love. I also admitted that she wasn't the BIGGEST reason I was choosing to move to LA. It was because I had big dreams, and they weren't going to come true in our small town of Sebring, Fl. I had just had a life-altering experience in the form of a health scare, and what better time than the present? Everything happens for a reason, and I realized that I had grown complacent. My health scare was exactly what I needed. It lit a fire underneath me to prompt me into action to live my best life, MY life, on my terms. I was never going to apologize for that. She understood, acknowledging that I was an adult, and while she didn't support my decision, God had revealed to her that this was part of his plan. Thanks, Big Dog, for smoothing that one over for me! My doctor's visit was great, which was welcoming news. I was diagnosed with my autoimmune disease in December of 2014, quit my office job in May of 2015, and was in California by July of the same year. I was beyond ecstatic to start a fresh new chapter in the city of Angels!

California was great, very challenging, but a challenge I welcomed. My mom called me almost every day to make sure I was alright and that I was eating. The job that I moved out there for wasn't supposed to start until 6 weeks after I got there, so I was in the midst of applying for other jobs. Eating, I will admit, was a little scarce at first. My dad got paid on Thursdays, so she would call the nearest Papa John's closest to me and order a pizza and a Pepsi. I rationed out that pizza for as long as I could! I finally got a job, and she didn't have to make sure I was eating something. I would keep her informed on what was happening with my music and acclimating to the big city. For the first time in my life, I felt alone by force. I am an introvert-extrovert, meaning that I love being social and around people, but I welcome my alone time. I crave it. I need it to function properly. Being alone was always my choice until I moved to one of the biggest cities in the world. I welcomed her numerous phone calls for once because it was some of the only genuine human interactions I had for a while. About a year into living in my new home, she told me that she was proud of me. That she admired the strength I had to chase my dreams unapologetically. In her eyes, I was fearless. She tearfully told me she never had such strength. She always wanted to be an interior designer, something she would have excelled at for sure. We never had a lot of money, but our homes always looked like something straight out of a catalog. That was something I learned from her. This was another time that I was left speechless because all I ever heard was how reckless I was and how I was going to fall flat on my face. I wasn't living in the purpose of God, so I wasn't going to amount to anything, which was always so hurtful because deep down, all I ever wanted to do was make her proud. To be a daughter she could brag about. The irony was I heard from practically everyone but her how proud she was of me, from her friends, her family, and church people. They were constantly vouching for her. Telling me that all she talked about was her beautiful daughter the singer. But why, WHY was it so hard for her to say those words to me? And what I did hear from her, why was it always so cruel? I really appreciated her saying that to me because what I was trying to achieve was no easy feat. A small-town girl with no money and no connections. I was trying to make so much happen all on my own. The least I could have from my parents was their emotional support and words of encouragement. I was at a loss for words yet again, and I know I didn't have the reaction that I should have had. My heart was closed off to her at this point. I had come to terms a long time ago that she was someone I was meant to love from afar. Our conversations seemed to be more productive and calmer when there was distance between us. I knew her health was declining, but she always managed to pull through so many times before. I became a little desensitized to her health issues, or maybe I was in denial. I had one chance to go back home while I lived on the west coast. I was saving money for my music. I had gotten a second job as well and it was one of the months that you get three paychecks, so I had enough for the month's bills and rent as well. I had a thought to buy a plane ticket home to visit my family. I chose to use that money towards a song that ended up being one of the worst songs I had produced. And to add insult to injury, I only got back $300 of the $1000 I paid because they still needed to get paid. I sent the song to my closest friends and other producers I was working with, and they all agreed with the extremely poor quality. I was beside myself. I worked very hard for my money. I ate ramen and pb&j's for weeks to save up that amount with nothing to show for it. The sad part was that it would have been the only time I could have made it back home before my mom passed in August of 2017.

Chapter 19

Moment of Truth...

Even though my mom had been sick for years, I never really thought she would die. She was one of the strongest people I knew, both mentally and physically. She would get dialysis in the morning and be helping someone by lunch and still would muster the strength to make it to church after dinner. She was always helping someone in some way. Whether it was organizing an event, helping someone file their immigration paperwork for citizenship, or watching someone's children. She would also make sure the house was cleaned and cooked for my dad and me most days. She was the best cook. I wished I had paid more attention to how she made things. She did write down her recipes somewhere, and I would give anything to find that little index card box she kept them in. I remember watching her in the hospital bed, staring at her, waiting for her to wake up. She had been on life support quite a few times, and she pulled through every single time. She was in the hospital this last time for a diabetic amputation. They were going to take the entire foot, but she somehow managed to convince them to take a few toes. She hated surgery because she would always have complications with the anesthesia. That one time in college when she was on life support, the doctors came to my dad and me and told us to prepare for her death after a slight complication after she went under. But she pulled through. I was aware of the last surgery, and I was praying for a smooth and quick recovery like always. She needed to be on breathing tubes again after the amputation, but she did manage to pull through. Once she was coherent enough, she had her best friend call me to tell me the good news. I was relieved, but I reminded her that she was still going to be permanently in a wheelchair, so she wouldn't be able to do as much as she was used to. I could hear her crying at the sound of my voice and laughing when I told her to essentially retire. My dad and her best friend kept telling her to stop trying to talk to me because she had tubes down her throat, and they could cause damage to her trachea. A few days later, she was released from the hospital, in a wheelchair, of course. Some of the people from church and her closest friends had a welcome home party for her. According to her best friend, she was so full of life that day. That night, she would get up in the middle of the night to do something. We weren't sure if it was to use the bathroom or go to sleep on the couch, where it was much cooler. She fell and hit her head, causing a traumatic brain injury. Her primary cause of death was a brain hemorrhage, but my mom's health had been declining for years. She once attempted to get on the kidney transplant list but was deemed ineligible due to a 12% health rating. She had heart, lung, and other issues caused by diabetes as well, so she wasn't even close to a qualified candidate. Despite this, she held on for years. She was put on life support until I was able to get on a plane and get home, which was the following day. I sat in her hospital room, stunned. I still couldn't believe such a force was gone. There was no way. She was going to pull through again. I waited for the doctor to come in because I wanted to make sure everything that could be done was done. He showed me her brain scans that registered no brain activity whatsoever and reassured me that no amount of time was going to make a difference. She was already gone, in a sense. All the plans had already been made before I got there.

They were going to "pull the plug" on Saturday, which just so happened to be my dad's birthday, and have the funeral on the following Tuesday. I hadn't cried yet. Not when I was told the news, not when they give the family time right before the nurses take out the breathing tubes, not even at her funeral. I was processing so many conflicting emotions. My mom and I had been through so much. She had caused me so much pain, both physically and emotionally. I remember every bruise, every nosebleed, every push against the wall, every slap across the face, every punch, all her hurtful words. And what hurt even more was that she knew what I had been through before I even came to live with her. She knew I was already so broken, so defeated. She was the person who almost gave the fatal blow. I couldn't ignore that. On the other hand, with age comes wisdom and understanding. I will never excuse nor condone her actions. However, seeing her own father backhand her across the face at the age of 50 once when he came to visit and watching this force of nature cower before him, filled me with such pity. I was in high school then, but if there was any time I wanted to disrespect my elders if you catch my drift, it was at that moment. Another sad piece to the puzzle that was my mother. Coupled with the fact that she lost her own mother at the age of 16 to breast cancer and was the eldest of 6, thus taking on a lot more responsibility than she should have had to, and seeing how her father was quick to use violence, she made a little more sense to me. She also once disclosed to me that the first man she was ever engaged to beat her so badly with a can of spray paint that she almost died. The figurative rod was all she knew. As I have said before, the cycle of domestic violence was a cycle for a reason.

I have always been the type of person to want to know why people are the way that they are. What makes them tick? When a person displays some form of negative behavior, I think to myself, hmm, why? When it is someone, I care for, I will do my best to find out to gain some understanding and best-case scenario in my mind, help them in some way be a better version of themselves. It makes all the difference sometimes to even be made aware. Not to toot my own horn, but I consider myself to be some very wise counsel. I have been through the ringer, and I am still standing. I was blessed with a copious amount of self-awareness, so I give some away at every chance I get because most people can't say the same...anyway. My mom. I was sitting in the empty church, still looking up at her casket. Everyone else was in the fellowship hall, enjoying the food and making remarks about how my mom's cooking was way better and if she would have been content with how her viewing was being handled because she was the hostess with the mostess! Our house was where everyone came to for the holidays, for church events, and for the random get-togethers. She was in her element planning parties and gatherings, making sure everything looked just right and everyone had enough to eat. Holidays haven't been the same without her. I was enjoying these remarks and all the stories, but I needed to be alone with my thoughts. And I was tired of being asked if I was ok and involuntarily getting hugged and pats on the back. Remember, I don't care for such things. I was particularly getting annoyed at people commenting on how they found it odd I hadn't cried at my own mother's viewing. I started to feel like I wasn't grieving in a socially acceptable way, and since I didn't feel like putting on a show, I went to sit in a pew a few rows back from her casket. It was fitting that I was in a church at that moment because I was convinced that the darkness was coming for me again.

I knew one thing to be true, that my mom was a praying woman, and I whole heartedly knew that she interceded on my behalf. I have always felt this dark cloud looming over me, just waiting for the second I let my guard down to take me over. My life, for the most part, was always filled with hardships and heartbreaks, crisis after crisis; it just never seemed to let up. As I grew older, I had to learn that my actions had consequences and that I was the cause of certain circumstances that came my way, but even my closest friends, who have known me for years, couldn't deny that I attracted misfortune. It's almost eerie. When I do know moments of peace, I cannot for the life of me let my guard down because I know the other shoe will drop at any time as it's always done. I couldn't even fathom what demons and tribulations were waiting for me now that I didn't have my mom in my corner. It was such a cruel joke of the universe to make the one person who cared and loved me the most one of the people in my life who caused me the most pain. The tears didn't come because I would go back and forth from grief and sadness due to her passing to anger and disdain because of the hurtful memories. What was always missing from my mom's mouth was an apology. An admittance of guilt.

Looking back, before I left for California, my mom and I had a lot of conversations to say the things that were left unsaid. I said them, but even when I poured my heart out or extended my apology, I never got that in return. And now, I never will. One of my exes came and sat with me. He was my first love and, before that, one of my best friends, so I could never hate him. I was glad of the company and even more glad that he wasn't expecting me to engage in conversation. He did comment how my sister showed me up by getting up on the pulpit and saying some kind words even though she hadn't known her like I did. She even sang a little song. I just didn't trust myself. I didn't trust that when I opened my mouth, nice and encouraging words would follow. A lot of people in that church knew what she had done to me and never once did anything to stop it. I also didn't trust that when I got up there, I wouldn't just break down in front of everyone. Fun fact about me, I get irrationally angry and annoyed at myself when I cry in front of people. It is something I should work on. But furthermore, not only did I not want to cry in front of that many people, but I also didn't want them to witness the meltdown that was sure to follow if I did. Our familial issues were no secret to almost everyone in attendance. Her friends.

Her family that could make it. The church members. It felt hypocritical of me to get up there and talk about how a great and loving person she was, because most times, that was not the person I saw.

The kicker was my mom was a great and loving person. She would give the shirt off her back, knowing that she only had one shirt left. She gave people money when we were getting the electricity and other bills cut off. She was donating to food banks and cooking meals when at times, we were recipients of the same charity. Her loyalty and dedication to God, despite the countless health battles and other hardships she endured, were commendable. Her faith never wavered. Often times, her intentions were pure, but the execution was off. Way off. I repeatedly had this conversation with her that if you are going to help someone, you can't control what they do with that help. Just because it wasn't the way you would have done things doesn't mean the other person was wrong. You give someone $20 for gas, that doesn't mean you get to ask them when and where they are going and dictate every mile. That was an ongoing theme. But one thing I have observed in her and other people is that the "control freaks" we come across are so controlling because they once felt so powerless. My mom had a very rough exterior, and speaking from personal experience, there was a valid reason for that. She held back a lot of pain, both physically and mentally. But as I've had to remind myself, the people around me aren't the cause of my pain, therefore shouldn't be the recipients of my wrath and unpleasantness. My dad and I received the brunt of that. While I know my dad will never admit this out loud, I'll say it for him: she was a lot, and I know he felt some sort of peace when she passed. She had a lot of redeemable qualities; I will give you that. She had a spirit and willingness to help others around her. Her strength and mental toughness were unmatched. That was perhaps what I admired most about her. As with my other mothers, she tried her best with the hand that she was dealt. My dad wasted no time in wanting all her things gone from the house, so I spent the next few days packing up her clothes and belongings which we donated to a local charity. I felt like I was trespassing. I came across the skeletons in her closet and was filled with even more sadness. Other pieces to the puzzle were being added. As I read through court documents and clippings of newspapers, I decided then and there to just let go. We all had secrets. We all had moments from our past that we wish would never come to light. She was fighting her own demons. Who was I to judge?

She was another person who would constantly point out that I chose to dwell on the bad and not acknowledge the good. I had the same answer; what happens when the bad far outweighs the good? What happens in the middle of the night when I can't sleep because when I do, my red memory plays in a loop, and my thoughts are plagued with images of blood on the walls or in bathtubs? What happens when I'm tearing myself to shreds because I gained 3 pounds, and her voice seeps back into my mind, playing in a loop of how fat and disgusting I am, and that in turn, will make me unworthy of love? Like I have stated before, I rarely doubt myself, but when I do, boy do I know how to pick myself apart and light those pieces on fire, and it's my mother's voice saying, "I told you so. I knew you wouldn't amount to anything. I knew you'd find a way to mess things up." Does our brain pick and choose which memories we hold onto? Which voices play louder in our heads? Is there a switch that can be turned off? I would like to know because I will not hesitate. What I can say is since my mom's passing, I have made more of an effort to let what's in the past stay in the past. Because what is the point now? I will only be hurting myself.

It's been a few years now. I had chosen to leave California to acclimatize my dad to his new role as a widower. Of course, I blamed my mom for that decision. That is when the anger-stage of grief hit me. Having to uproot my life. Having to move back to my hometown I so desperately hated. Not having a mother at my wedding. She would have loved that. Now, there would be no Abuelita (grandmother) for my children. Those kids would have been spoiled rotten. A running joke between my dad and I is that it was a good thing I was a decent human being because he was no disciplinarian! And what about my dreams? I had every intention of moving back to the West Coast, but then Covid happened shortly after. One thing no one tells you is how many times you have to put your own dreams on hold because life simply happens. That wasn't her fault, clearly. While the initial sting of losing a parent has passed, I can't deny that her absence is missed. My dad is now remarried. And all I will say is I wasn't prepared for this version of him. I have gotten used to the holidays away from home. I have decided to just start my own traditions with friends who are in similar situations. I am also trying to figure out where home is since I have nothing left for me in Florida. Going from place to place, city to city has grown wearisome to me. I just want to be home. I just want to feel at home feel at peace with myself and my surroundings, which has been hard for me. I recently moved to Denver, Co. I like it more than I thought, and because I don't hate it, I have decided to stay put and just be. Quit running, from what I have yet to figure out. As one can imagine, moving to a new state presented its challenges. Things didn't go as planned, which was no surprise there, but the person I wanted to call was my mom. I just wished I had her praying for me. She was a praying woman, and I know God listened to her. I've realized lately that she was the one person that truly cared about me. She had a funny way of showing it at times, I will admit, but she loved me and cared about me more than anyone else in this world. She tried her best. I know that. She has been forgiven just as I told Dee that I forgave her. But despite all that, I feel so incredibly alone in this chapter of my life, and I wish I had my mom to call. I know what she would tell me. I'm strong enough to get through anything, which is something she always admired in me. But sometimes, I'm tired of being strong. And in the very few moments in my life where I didn't want to be the strong one for once, I had her strength. And without it, it all falls on me. With recent events, I have felt that pressure and how I took for granted those times that she carried me and let me rest. Let me build my strength back up to keep going. I am my mother's daughter. I am resilient. I am resourceful. I am brave. As she pointed out repeatedly, I am ridiculously stubborn (ok pot, way to call the kettle black on that one, mom, just saying), but the universe loves a stubborn heart because we are the ones that will not give up. We're relentless in our pursuits of what sets our souls on fire! The rewards are great for people like me, and it saddens me that she will not be here when I accomplish everything I set out to do.

At the end of the day, daughters just want to please their mothers, and I am no different. We fought a lot because we were one and the same: stubborn, passionate, and had a need always to be right! I take pride in the fact that in every space I have inhabited, I always get compliments on my talent for color, décor, and use of space like my mama! In another life, I would have pursued interior design like she had wanted to. I take pride in a clean home. I will admit that my cleanliness is a slight compulsion, but we blame the parents for everything, am I right? I take pride in the fact that I am constantly complimented on my appearance. Not in a vain way, but because I try to look presentable most days with nice clothes and hair and makeup done like she taught me. Don't get it twisted; I know she shakes her head up in heaven at the times I leave my apartment looking like I ask young girls if they'd like a random apple that's totally not poisonous, but I regret nothing! Most importantly, I take pride in the passion I have for people, which is something I learned from her. I saw It every day, I could never deny that. She was passionate about her family, her friends, the church members, and every child she encountered. She was always buying toys or clothes for the kids in her life. Over here acting like Santa Clause! But the child she cared for the most was me. The child that she loved most was me. In truth, she saved me. Who knows what my life would have looked like or how I would have turned out if it weren't for her? Despite everything, I am grateful because I know I wouldn't be the woman I am today if it wasn't for her.

ME

(Yikes)

Chapter 20

I just need to say this. I can't blame every single problem I have ever had in my life on my mother(s). I am my own person. I fly. I sore. I crash...all by myself. However, there was a slight theme in my maternal figures that I couldn't deny. Now, one can say that the only common denominator in all 3 situations was me, and therefore, I must have been the issue, but I stand by what I said, children are blameless. I look back on my childhood, and a pattern was there: a pattern of abuse, abandonment, and neglect. I countered that with a pattern of my own: a pattern of strong will, defiance, and anger, and boy was I angry. As I was writing the last few chapters of my book, I really started to wonder, where did all my anger come from? Maybe she's born with it, or maybe it's mommy issues! I made the unfortunate mistake of googling signs that a woman has mommy issues once, and it was like looking in the mirror: trust and intimacy issues, demanding, controlling, fear of abandonment, trouble forming an attachment (sigh...not with this again), trouble expressing themselves emotionally, so on and so forth. Ok, fine, guilty. Geeze. Hey, in my defense, I could have been worse. I could have been a man with mommy issues, that list looked profoundly different...and was riddled with some of the most prolific serial killers of all time, but I digress. I took a step away from my book for a while because I couldn't really find the words to explain the key ingredient in the part I played in my own childhood dysfunction. One night, I was having trouble sleeping so I did what every other human being does when they can't sleep: shamelessly scroll Amazon and add things they don't need to their shopping cart. In my list of suggested items was a book called, "Why are you full of rage? Because you are full of grief." -Anne Carson, Grief Lessons: Four Plays by Euripides. I looked up at the ceiling, a.k.a. God, and smirked. Touche, universe, touché. In the same week, while taking the bus to work, I was looking to kill some time off the commute by looking at Instagram, and I came across this quote: "I sat with my anger long enough until she told me her real name was grief." -C.S. Lewis. If I hadn't received the message the first time, it was now crystal clear. I was so angry because I was grief-stricken. I came into this world already at a loss, absent a mother and a father, a family. Love. A sense of security. And it only got worse from there. I won't lie; being rehomed as many times as I was really did a number on me. That is one thing my adoptive mother never understood. I have never met someone else who grew up in foster care and had that scenario happen to them because I would like to know how they feel about it and how they managed to cope. Some wounds are deeper than others, and that is one of my deepest. I have had the hope of a loving family dangled in front of me just to have it ripped away in the cruelest of ways so many times that I finally just lost hope altogether, and I will admit, my last family felt that. Like I have said before, I was made to be the villain since birth, when in actuality, I was a victim but was never treated as such. I often wonder how different things could have been for me, had I been treated with softness and kindness, patience and understanding. I guess that concept is now called "gentle parenting" and who knows if that would have worked on a child like me. One thing I do know is that I didn't ask for any of it. I didn't ask for a birth mother who was incapable of keeping me and giving me the life I deserved. I didn't ask for adoptive parents who weren't equipped with the tools and/or the knowledge to care for a child like me and um, didn't care enough to educate themselves or ask for help because that was always an option instead of rehoming me over and over again. I didn't ask to be sexually abused. I didn't ask to be beaten repeatedly because, make no mistake, I wasn't "disciplined" or "reprimanded" in the name of the Lord; I was left bruised and bloodied on multiple occasions. I had every reason to be angry. I had every reason to lash out. I HAVE every reason to be exactly the way that I am, for good or bad.

Grief. Mystery solved! I was in a constant state of grieving. No, I AM in a constant state of grieving. I'm going to drop a truth bomb, trauma never leaves you, you just manage it and hopefully learn healthy coping mechanisms. They say there are 5 stages of grief: denial, anger, bargaining, depression, and acceptance. Wow, my life is making even more sense as I write this. Let's start off with the first stage: Denial. Ignorance is bliss, isn't it? I have mastered the art of compartmentalizing my emotions. My circumstances wouldn't be real if I didn't think about them. When I was younger, I believed that my adoptive family was coming back for me despite the multiple actions to suggest otherwise.

I couldn't admit to myself that they didn't want me. When I moved to Florida and had to start school with new peers, I would lie that I had met my birth parents and that they, at some point, were coming back for me as well. I simply could not accept my abandonment. Or my ego could not accept that I was worth abandoning, ouch. It wasn't until I got to high school that I stopped lying. Why was I embarrassed over circumstances I had no control over? Why was I embarrassed of my birth mom being a drug addict and a prostitute when she was her own person? Why was I embarrassed that I was adopted? Why was I embarrassed about being put in a children's home? Why was I embarrassed that I was given away and placed with yet another family? But as I dug deeper, embarrassment wasn't what I was feeling. It was a shame. I was ashamed. I think I can say with certainty that most of us have felt shame over one thing or the other, and it is a ruthless emotion. Shame proves hard to sit with even for grown adults, and I was a child. A teenager. So, I denied it, denied it all. People look at you differently. They just do. If my peers couldn't even understand why I didn't look like my parents or why we'd have different last names, how could they comprehend the whole story? But the older I got, the more I realized that it wasn't their story to comprehend in the first place. If I were going to be looked at or treated differently, then so be it. If someone couldn't digest my truth, they were free to choke on it. So, I stopped denying my past, specifically my childhood. I'm not one to volunteer information, but if someone had a question or was curious, I would answer if I felt comfortable. That too, came with time.

Anger. I used to want to hide from the world. To disappear. I would have given anything to be invisible because I felt too damaged to exist. To always be branded as the broken, the worthless, the loose cannon, the girl with too much fire who would forever be consumed by it. Unable to control her rage. I used to try to convince myself that I wanted to be alone. For a time, I tried to hide myself away for everyone else's protection, but the older I get, I need to hide myself away from those very same people for MY protection. One of my more dominating traits is my natural rebellious spirit. I have never cared much for people-pleasing. But that stems from doing my best, being my best, emulating the same behavior I saw other kids doing that were considered the "good ones," and it still not being enough. I still wasn't enough to keep my family happy. I still wasn't enough to keep a family, period. Or maybe I was just too much. Yes, that's it. I always seemed to be too much. I tried. I tried so hard to be good. I tried so hard to be on my best behavior. I tried to be like the little girls I saw with the pretty dresses and the happy dispositions. Giggling and smiling. But honestly, what did I have to be smiling about? At that age, I was too young to understand the concept of "fake it to you make it." What would end up happening is that I still got sent away. I still got abused in some way. So, I stopped caring, especially when it came to authority figures. I met my match in Ruthie, the woman I consider my mom because she gave me no room to move, to breathe, or to just be. She also added a little razzle-dazzle, I like to call religion, to the mix. Now, my rebellion was considered sinful. I was deemed the spawn of Satan, a demon child, just an overall bad seed. I was just born bad. Ooo, challenge accepted! I fell into my villain role because that was all that was expected of me, nothing more, nothing less. Fun fact about me, as you may have figured out by now, I'm a writer. I write songs and blog posts, I hope to write other books, and I want to get back to finishing my screenplays. Basically, I'm a natural-born storyteller. The stories that I find intriguing and honestly gravitate towards are the villain arcs. I know how shocking. But it isn't just me; take a look at Hollywood! Cinema and television are obsessed with what it is to be bad! But the formula is the same, isn't it? Someone suffers immense pain and loss, grieve, and take it out on the world in the most destructive of ways. Villains live life on their own terms, damming the consequences. It is, in some cases, freeing. Modern society also has an obsession with true crime documentaries, myself included, but I always roll my eyes when they speak about childhood. Often, the story is the same. They were adopted, grew up in foster care, and mistreated by parents and/or parental figures. It became the staple in every Criminal Minds episode. While I would get annoyed, I would count myself fortunate because while some of those stories were fiction, a lot of them were not. I know firsthand what that anger and pain feels like. I have felt that darkness, that despair. That sense of hopelessness. I have been tempted to turn off that switch and lose my humanity. But this wasn't the movies. I wouldn't be given a redemptive arc. There would be no possibility of a happy ending. My choices would have real-life consequences, and my ending would be that I would be alone, in jail, on drugs, or dead. I knew that wasn't the ending I wanted for me, so I promised myself that I would do better. Be better. Now, there wasn't a formula that I followed to suddenly be a ray of sunshine. Like Bruce Banner in the Avengers once said, "That's my secret Captain; I'm always angry." (yes, I just quoted The Hulk, get over it because I'm about to do it again!) That fire is always there, bubbling beneath the surface. It doesn't let up; it doesn't dim. It didn't just magically disappear one day, but what did happen is that I did this little thing called maturing. I grew up and out of my behavioral issues. I had things in my life, and people I cared about that were too important to lose. I found music my biggest coping mechanism and the greatest way to keep that fire manageable. I swim. I bike. I hit the weight room when I need to point that fire at something outside of myself. But The Hulk also said, "What I realized later was that my anger wasn't my weakness; it was actually my strength; I just needed to control it and use it." I did grow up, and I am still a villain, but a societal villain! I am an outspoken woman of color with my own thoughts and opinions, and I am sure as hell not afraid to express them. I am confident in my own skin, standing tall at 5 feet 8 inches. I am fuller-figured, being a size 14. I have big, natural hair. I defy societal beauty standards and have made it my mission to help women of all shapes and sizes do the same. I am confident in my sexuality. I am wise and intelligent. These attributes automatically villainized me as a grown woman, but what the world didn't know was that I was already used to playing that part! I have felt that pressure, that scrutiny and I remain unfazed and grounded. Unshakable. It made me find my power. My voice. It gave birth to my greatest passion, my passion for people, especially those who have been written off by society for some reason or another. The underdogs. I will forever strive to be their mouthpiece. Their biggest cheerleader. Their champion. I have been trying to keep my cliches to a minimum, but I will say this one: diamonds are just rocks forged under immense heat and pressure. And that is what I became. A diamond.

Chapter 21

The other stages of grief were abundantly clear when I reflected upon my life. The stage of depression, not so much. Or so I thought. This one is where I feel the most vulnerable. To say reflecting on my childhood trauma depresses me is a given. I don't think that comes as much of a surprise. To say that I still have nightmares, sleepless nights, tearful emotional episodes, or moments were I break down because of my childhood is...expected. Right? I get seasonally depressed around the holidays as well because it reminds me of all I have lost and missed out on. It also reminds me of my mom (mom #3) and her passing. Holidays haven't been the same without her. Ok, great; I wrapped that stage up rather quickly.... until I had a moment of extreme honesty with myself. I have always deemed my pride as my most toxic trait. But my pride only affects me. Maybe I'll rephrase and say it's one of my most masochistic traits. So, the trait that takes the cake, then, would be my ability to shut. down. Emotionally check out. I have garnered the worst of reactions, even worse than when I blow up or argue back when I serve my pursed lips and blank stare. I was told once by a friend that it was so aggravating because one could see the exact moment on my face when I mentally checked out of a conversation. The wall went up and there was no reaching me after that point. I have also mastered the art of figuratively disappearing off the face of the earth. There is a popular term called "ghosting," which means you just never hear or see someone again. It is typically used in pop culture regarding dating. Back in my dating app days, I ghosted plenty of men. I have ghosted a few people in my life that I shouldn't have, and I can only hope that they forgive me for that. Now, I will never claim to be a trendsetter, but during college, before "ghosting" became a thing, I coined the phrase going ghost, or that I was in ghost-mode. Basically, it was my way of telling the people around me that I had planned on staying home, not answering my phone, and keeping my engagement to a minimum. I did this so much that others around me started to say they were "pulling a Lauren and going ghost." I would do this for valid reasons, studying for finals or not going out with my friends so much to save money. I would also do this at the first sight of any emotional turbulence. I would essentially hide myself away. The problem with this was that the people that cared about me the most would start to worry. I wouldn't answer their calls. I wouldn't even answer the door when they tried to make sure I was still alive, at least. I am a stress-internalizer. I also internalize my emotions. That is how I have gotten through every hardship in my life. I put my head down, and I work through it, most times, all on my own. I was rarely consoled for crying. As a matter of fact, I was punished. Showing emotion period seemed to have negative consequences for me, so I trained myself to stay in a very small spectrum of emotion, careful not to get too high (like feeling joy, excitement, or love), but also weary of the low (sadness, anger, or even disappointment). I think that's why, oftentimes, I come off as cold or distant. And it was true; I did have trouble expressing emotions because I seemed to have always been doing it in an unacceptable manner. A lot of times, I didn't have the emotional responses that were deemed socially appropriate, and it was mentally exhausting for me to try to figure it out at the moment to avoid the awkward pauses and blank stares I would often get from those around me. The consequences, again, were severe if I got it wrong, which, let's just say, happened way more than me getting it right. I was left. I was sent away. I was beaten. I pride myself on being able to hold myself together. I am the rock. I am one of the strong ones. I bounce back rather quickly. I had built a coat of armor that was impenetrable. One of my current favorite shows is called Bridgerton. I have also purchased all the books and have read most of them. I love period pieces, and Shonda Rimes is absolutely brilliant in the modern spin she has put on the books. There is a scene where Violet, the mother, is talking to one of her sons about putting on this façade that he is someone he's not for fear of letting someone see the real him. She says, "I do not blame you for putting on armor lately. But you must be careful that the armor does not rust and set so that you might never be able to take it off." -Violet Bridgerton. That quote hit me like a ton of bricks. It brought me back to the time when I almost lost everyone in my life because my walls were built so high that no one could climb over them to see the real me.

In my mid-20s, it all caught up to me. My armor was beginning to rust. I was emotionally unavailable and, therefore, attracted my fair share of ill-suited partners. I would joke that my greatest dating advice was that you can't get left if you're not there to begin with. People would laugh and agree but really take in what I was actually saying. Dating was always hard for me. Not because I didn't attract men, that was never my problem. But because I had to grow up fast. What my generation seemed to fixate on were trivial things in my mind, so I struggled to make meaningful connections. What I valued was just different. What I chose to spend my energy on was just different. I also struggled with being vulnerable and opening up. If I had a dollar every time I heard that from a man... The hookup culture was perfect for someone like me because all I had to give was my body, a physical presence. "Situationships" worked well because they were basically relationships without the commitment or emotional investment. I could do that. Opening up about my past was hard. It was considered too heavy for most, and I understood that. I never judged anyone when they said it was too much for them. I couldn't change it anyway. And the thing is, I've only really been hurt by those closest to me because they possessed the tools to do so. One would think that if someone cares for you, they wouldn't want to inflict the same pain on the wounds that were taking more time to heal. I had learned a long time ago not to cross the line in arguments or disagreements with people I cared about because things will blow over, and you may even forgive each other, but those low blows and hurtful words linger in the back of one's mind and slowly chip away at the foundation of a friendship or relationship, until one day, the final blow is made and irreparable damage has been caused. So, I chose not to give my secrets away. No harm could be done if they didn't possess the ammunition. So here I was, finding even more reasons to hide myself away. To become a recluse. I did everything within my power to stay within my small spectrum of emotion, and for the longest time, I succeeded, but at what cost? I couldn't be abandoned if I wasn't there to abandon. Check. Didn't have to worry about intimacy if I never let anyone close enough. Check. Didn't have to worry about being hurt if I didn't let anyone in to know what could truly hurt me. Check. Sounds...lonely. And it was, but being alone has never really bothered me. I enjoy my solitude. In fact, I crave it; I need it to function. For the longest time, I was numb. Or at least I was trying to be. I had men, good men, trying to get to know me and I wouldn't allow it. I remember many nights lying in bed, staring at the ceiling, and internally screaming at myself to feel something. To care. And the thing is, I did care, just not enough to show it. Prime emotional unavailability. I wanted to; I just didn't know how. If I let my guard down to feel romantically, I was sure the floodgates would open to let out all that I had managed to suppress. The good. The bad. The ugly. The brilliant. The beautiful. My darkness, My light. It would all be too much. And I remember what happened when I was deemed too much. Again, I get left. I got sent away. I was physically and emotionally abused. See, in those moments where I disappear and I hide from the world; it isn't me that I don't want anyone to see. It's that little girl who was starved for love who had managed to come to the surface. But she was never alone. She also brought her life-long companions: Self-loathing. Unworthiness. Doubt. My super small spectrum of emotion was where I felt comfortable, anything beyond it and I would panic and go running to the comfort of solitude. The few times I allowed myself to test the waters of what it would be like to be with someone, my self-sabotaging tendencies would get in the way. I would shut down. I was just no good at dating. At letting someone in. I could not bear for anyone to see me like that. Anyone. I am the rock. I am the strong one. I am not the one who shows weakness. But that little girl brings me to my knees every time. And that is why my relationships, both romantic and non-romantic, suffered. My friendships. Something had to give.

I didn't get into my first official adult relationship until I was 26 years old. I will always be thankful for my first love. Up until that point, I thought I was hopeless, destined to live a life alone of my own volition. I had no one to blame but myself. Maybe I cheated the system the first time around because the first man I fell in love with was already one of my closest friends. I already loved him, just in a different way, so making that transition to lovers seemed effortless. Now, I'll spare you the details, but we didn't end up together, I know how sad. That is a different story for another time. But it was the first time in my life that I allowed myself to take that emotional leap. To just let myself feel, which the joke has always been on me because I feel so deeply. I just suppress, suppress, suppress! This was my chance to prove to myself that I was capable of not running away. And I didn't. I also proved that I was able to withstand extreme emotion without it breaking me. Now, I loved my ex dearly, but he was the type of person who went for the deadliest of blows in an argument. Like using my mom's words against me. Using my past traumas against me. Darling, that's a big no-no in my book on both fronts. Or somehow making a confident woman feel like crap about herself. Or choosing to figuratively "leave" at the first legitimate disagreement. Or constantly being told it was too much to love me. It was too intense. The highs were too high, and the lows were too low. Doesn't this sound familiar? Basically, he deliberately hit me where it hurt emotionally, and I survived. Now, a heartbreak is a heartbreak, especially the first one, but I. survived. He is a good person, and he has his own set of issues to work through, but the biggest takeaway from our relationship was that I could love someone. I was capable of the level of vulnerability it takes to make that commitment. He also brought all my faults to light, and instead of beating myself up about them and wanting to hide away like I would normally do, I realized that yes, I'm a flawed human, but I'm still pretty awesome (I'm a little biased, obviously)! I was still worthy of love. Who I was, was ok. Even if I was deemed too much, too little, too whatever. It didn't take away from the fact that my good qualities still outweighed the bad by a landslide. And that was something I needed to figure out for myself. Around my first heartbreak was when my mom died as well. I was also in one of the biggest cities in the world, trying to make my wildest dreams come true. I was feeling the pressure. I was feeling the old reclusive habits returning. One of the biggest wakeup calls I had in my adult life was how very little my best friends and the man I still loved reached out to me during my mom's passing. It hurt me. In a passive-aggressive moment, I mentioned to one of my best friends at the time how I was a little disappointed that she wasn't calling me more to just see how I was fairing. Without hesitation, she told me it was because I never picked up the phone. I rarely answered texts. When I did reply, I would say that I was fine. That would be that. I would shut down. I was unknowingly pushing away the people I cared for the most. I couldn't complain. This was my doing. I had created a pattern of behavior that not only hurt me, but I was hurting those closest to me by always keeping them at arm's length. I vowed to do differently. To be different. I was weathered and heartbroken at the time, but once I was further along on my healing journey, I made it a point to be present. Present in the moment. Present in people's lives. Just present. I had one foot in the past and one foot in the future. I have always been fixated on the future. Fixated on making something of myself so I wouldn't be what everyone expected me to be. But in doing so, I was losing out on so much in the moment with people who already loved and cherished me as is. I was fighting ghosts. I held the opinions of people who weren't even in my life anymore above the ones who were. I needed to step outside of myself again. That started with me answering the damn phone when my friends would call! Communicating like the adult I was! Making it a priority to make sure I reached out as well. Not shutting down when I was going through something and facing it head on. Confiding in the people who loved me and trusting that they had my best interest at heart. Trusting that they'd still love me when I took off the mask and let them see all of me. I couldn't keep hiding myself away like I was doing because the only future that would bring me would be a future of loneliness; I knew that for certain.

Love would find me again at the age of 29. It was unexpected and unconventional, to be sure, but a nice surprise. My lessons in vulnerability were paying off, and I was open to letting someone get close to me. For the first time in my life, I experienced what it truly felt like to be seen. All facets of myself were fiercely on display as I was nearing the Dirty 30s! All the work I had been doing, both internally and externally, was paying off, and I wholeheartedly loved the version of myself I was becoming. I was set in my purpose. I was healing. I was vibrant. Encountering a man who looked at me in awe, and when he said he was proud of me, I could read his face to know he genuinely meant it, changed my life for the better. Meeting someone who had patience with me, especially in the beginning, was priceless. That wasn't something I had experienced before. While I had come along way, I wasn't where I wanted to be yet, and I had bouts of emotional distance and added a little sprinkle here and there of self-sabotaging tendencies. But he read me like a book and still decided to stay. I'm not perfect; he spoke his mind and let me know when I did or said something he didn't like, but he did it in a level-headed manner, and I respected that. This will come as a shock to absolutely no one, but I can be a brat at times. To have a man provide stern correction without berating, belittling, or dehumanizing me was refreshing. See, I did respond well to patience, love, and understanding. I trusted him with my life. He never once made me feel like I was too much like I had to dim my light or shrink myself to appease him. He never once made me feel like I had to apologize for my fire or for being overly passionate. He was privy to my light but also my darkness and never once looked at me differently. As we grew closer, the walls started to come down, and I shared a lot of my story with him. Shared my secrets. My hopes and my dreams. Now, it wasn't dealt in our cards for us to make it for the long haul, but I wouldn't regret our time together for anything. It was never less than a privilege to have him in my life. I won't lie, he set the bar super high for the next man that enters my life. But he set the bar high even for me. He challenged me. He helped me discover parts of myself that I had yet to see. He showed me that I was ready for love and, even more importantly, to BE loved. We had our sets of issues, but he gave me hope. Hope that it was possible to find the unconditional love and acceptance that I deserved. I didn't need to shun myself. I am enough. I am worthy, even on my bad days.

Chapter 22

Acceptance. Wow, where to begin on this one. Well, for starters, I had to accept that my circumstances were real, right? I had been abandoned ten times over. I was brought into this world the way that I was. I would most likely never meet my birth parents. My adoptive parents and/or family will forever remain in the background, in the shadows of my life. Those are choices we are making on both sides. As the outcast, the black sheep of the family, I do not see where I would be the one to reach out and form/maintain a relationship. That will be an issue I will not be the bigger person on, I'm sorry (not sorry). I had to accept that I was indeed a victim of mental, emotional, sexual, and physical abuse. I also had to accept that I was a child, and there was very little that I could have personally done to prevent what happened to me. I needed to stop blaming myself. I needed to let the shame go. I had nothing to be ashamed of. For the longest time, I held such animosity towards my younger self, as if she were a separate entity. Why didn't she fight back? Why couldn't she just be what everyone else wanted her to be? Why did she have to question every little thing? Why did she make everyone constantly want to desert her? WHY DIDN'T SHE FIGHT BACK? I hated her. Major ouch. Forgiving others is easy at times, isn't it? But why is it so hard to forgive ourselves? Why can't we come with the same amount of compassion and understanding and extend it inward? It is easy to blame someone else for your own problems, your own failures. I had to accept that I was she. She is me. Saying that I hated her, I had to admit that what I was REALLY saying was that I hated myself. Biggest. Ouch. Ever. That, my friends, is the wound that cuts the deepest, and it's the greatest, most powerful demon I face: self-loathing. Now, I mean it when I say I am my biggest fan. No one will ever know just how much work I have done to become this version of myself. I love myself, and I think I'm great! But it took me most of my life to get to this point because, in the same breath, I am most definitely my worst critic. I had to admit that one of those deprecating voices in my head was my own. I've been told repeatedly that the thing people tend to notice about me instantly is my confidence. I love that. I also have been asked many times where my confidence comes from, and I say the same thing. No one can say anything to me that I haven't said to myself, but 10 times worse. So, I am unbothered. Very few opinions truly matter to me. I make it a point to always walk with my head held high. I mean, all the world is a runway if you're fierce enough, and I am nothing if not fierce! But on a serious note, I do that because, for too long, I walked around like a wounded animal. I was upset that no one understood me or what I had been through. Could no one seriously show any sympathy towards me? At the time, I wouldn't allow myself to be seen as a victim, but I sure as hell wanted to be treated like one, and the irony in that fact was that I would never quite get to that point. To be treated with softness and kindness. To maybe have space held for me and my anger, which I recently found out was just grief in disguise. But I couldn't change the past. I couldn't press a magic button and have a different childhood. I have been through a lot and suffered much, but the biggest thing I had to accept was that I was entirely responsible for the rest of my life.

This is a tough pill to swallow, but sometimes, you just have to let it go. I just had to let it go! I am in no way, shape, or form invalidating my own feelings or trying to make light of my situation, but I had to stop living in the past. My greatest passion will always be music. It has been my lifeline. It will be something that I always include in my life because I fear who I would be without it. There was this one voice teacher during a lesson who stopped me dead in my tracks and asked me why I was up on that stage. Why did I want to be successful? I was honest and said I wanted to put on a good show and wanted people to like me and feel entertained because that would inevitably pay my bills and bring me success. I wanted to be successful because I had something to prove. He again stopped me and said, "Do you realize that all those answers had nothing to do with you? It's always about someone else. Get up on that stage because you have something to say! You have something you want others to feel. You should want to be successful for you. You should only have something to prove to yourself." I had the biggest chip on my shoulder because I was so worried about people who weren't even in my life anymore. I was still hung up on them, wanting to see what they missed out on. This is hard to say out loud, but I guarantee you these very people who used to keep me up at night don't even think about me at all. I'm talking about my adoptive family, old foster families, and case workers who had written me off. Friends and church people of my mom's. The people who had deemed me the lost cause. What I realized was that I needed to prove to MYSELF that I wasn't a lost cause. The opinion I had of myself was the most important. Changing my entire mindset made a difference in how I not only saw myself but it made me want to work harder because I was doing this for me! I just needed to get out of my own way. I could have used my childhood trauma as a crutch, as an excuse for my bad behavior. But I'm all about changing the narrative, so I chose to use it as a stepping stone to do some good in this world. To come into my purpose and be a beacon of hope. How on brand for me and my rebellious nature! A lot of my friends here in Denver are big into astrology. Back in my day, you just had the sign you were born with. I am an Aquarius. Very much so if you believe in that sort of thing. These same friends are dying for me to find out when I was born because now, you can essentially map out your entire life simply by knowing the time, date, and place of your birth. How bizarre! But hey, if the stars can affect the tides and steer explorers across oceans, who's to say they can't affect your life? Anyway, a friend came over one day to attempt to read my birth chart with what little information I could give her. Admittedly, I found a lot of the reading to be broad and very susceptible to interpretation, but something she said hit me right in the heart to the point where I teared up. An ongoing theme in my birth chart was the asteroid Chiron. When diving deeper (on the internet), in astrology, Chiron symbolizes unhealed injuries and incurable trauma. What? Because my Chiron was in Cancer (just go with me on this), these injuries and trauma were said to have been caused by family, specifically, parents who they felt didn't show them love, care, and a sense of security...mind blown! But what my birth chart said next was why I suddenly felt the need to be hugged. It said that if I could find a way to not drown in my own suffering, my own trauma, I could become something known as a wounded healer and help others with their trauma and healing. That folks, is what I needed to accept the most. That there was a purpose to my pain and suffering. There was a method to the universe's madness. It wasn't an accident of nature for me to go through all I've been through. If you believe in Jesus Christ, it has been prophesied over me that I was meant to impact others on a grander scale. I also had a gypsy woman who claimed to have been drawn to my place of work at the time because of my kindness and good spirit. She was new to town and needed help with ordering business cards and setting up her website. She didn't know that I had just graduated college with a degree in Public Relations and Marketing and just learned the skills to help her. She was a fortune teller and paid me with a free reading. Now, my Christian guilt kicked in, and I instantly refused, but my curiosity got the best of me. Her reading of my future was literally word for word of the prophecy that had been said to me at a church convention over a decade prior! And apparently, it's even written in the stars! It's kind of an oxymoron to say that your life isn't about you, but it's your life; of course it is! I find comfort in knowing that the constant trials that I have faced could be used to help others find their own strength. Life didn't end when I was left at the group home in Tennessee. Life didn't end when I had to wipe my own blood off the bathroom floor in Florida. Life didn't end when my heart was broken for the first time in California. It has taken a lot of personal growth and healing to rid myself of the shame and guilt I carried for years, so therefore, I am not ashamed to admit that as a 34-year-old woman, I still cry myself to sleep at times. I still lie awake, wishing that things could have been different for me. I still get lost in my own reflection in the mirror, and I have to snap myself out of it and remind myself that I am worthy. I am worthy of all the goodness and light this world can give me. I am worthy of love, of peace. I. am. worthy. I still have to turn the music up in my headphones sometimes because those voices are talking a little louder than usual. I still have moments where my heart is just a little too heavy, and I want to give up. But then I remember my purpose my calling, and it gives me the strength to keep on going. While I am one tough broad, I didn't get here all on my own. I had good people in every chapter of my life, reminding me that I could do better and be better. I can't give up because I have people to uplift and inspire. See, while most villains come from tragic backgrounds, so do superheroes. Which one you become is all contingent on the choices you make. I am in charge of my own redemptive arc. As one of my acquaintances once said, "I have faith in God and the universe, but my confidence will always lie within myself." So, stay tuned. It's going to be big!

Chapter 23

My very own Moment of Truth...

My buzzword for 2024 was "intention." To take a step back and dive deeper into my actions. My words. To truly understand my "why". I know myself pretty well, but there is always room for improvement, and sometimes those improvements are reminders. Opportunities to keep ourselves centered. Grounded. On track. I have examined and assessed my intentions for this book over and over, making sure I am aligning myself with my purpose. And I whole-heartedly believe I have taken the right steps to put me on the path to achieve what I was put on this earth to do. Hell, I dove headfirst into it! It brought me back to one of those last conversations I had with my mom before she passed. She was commending me on how fearless I was. I remember telling her that no one is truly without fear. That I was terrified, I was just too damn stubborn to give up. We laughed because I am nothing, if not bullheaded, and we both knew it. It is kind of what I'm known for…unfortunately. What was seen as bravery was just pride wrapped in a sparkly cheetah print bow. I have once again been deemed brave, and this time, I wear that title as a badge of honor. Writing this book is perhaps the most vulnerable I have ever been. To bear my scars and remove the mask and just stand still…on display for the world to see. I am not running. I am not hiding. I am keeping my head high and fixing my crown. Even with the tears flowing and my hands trembling. Even with every negative emotion I have spent decades suppressing, rushing to the surface and pouring out of me. My grief. My shame. My self-loathing. My rage. I let it flow and flow until I was engulfed in familiar territory: the darkness. But I read somewhere that if you find yourself constantly surrounded by darkness, have you ever stopped to think that maybe it's because you're the source of light? I have spent too much of my life thinking there was something fundamentally wrong with me, and it wasn't just because I had an unpleasant childhood. Too easy, people! But because…I feel at ease in the darkness. At home even. I relish and thrive in it. I seek it out as a place of comfort and solace. But to be utterly consumed by the light! To let it radiate within and out of me, what a remarkable feeling that is too. And that is when it hit me. I was both. Darkness and Light. So, when I removed the mask, why would I always think that what was left to be seen was something hideous or pitiful? That what was pouring out of me was to be eluded? A deadly virus needing containment or such a volatile force that was to be sent away to the outermost corners of the earth. Taking off my mask and revealing my scars would, in fact, unleash something that those around me would absolutely feel: my inner fire. That unstable flame. The key component in my most destructive behavior. But doesn't fire also bring warmth and comfort? Isn't one of its primary purposes to...illuminate?

Writing this book was my closure. Finally, having the will and mental strength to sit down with my pain has shifted my perspective on how I view my shortcomings. My failures. My weaknesses. I am not perfect. I have never pretended to be as such. And that is ok. More than ok, in fact, because my weaknesses go hand in hand with my strengths. My light couldn't exist without my darkness, and I have been doing myself a disservice by choosing to hide. Putting up my walls and never taking off the mask. In doing so, I not only hid away the bad, but I hid away the good in me as well, and trust me when I say there has always been far more good, even more than I give myself credit for. Denying my past. Ignoring my pain. Staying silent. Shutting down as a defense mechanism. Not sharing my story. These were the ways I hid, and I am through with hiding. Writing this book made me see myself a little clearer. When I look into the mirror and gaze at my reflection, I still see my scars, both inward and outward, but I now see how they complement my beauty that resides in the same places. When I peer into my soul, I see that fire, ablaze and unruly, illuminating eyes that display my passion for people and the need to fill the world with more art and ingenuity. More compassion and understanding. More love, and not the love spoken about in hallmark cards, but the kind of love without terms or conditions. The kind of love that moves mountains and softens even the hardest of hearts. The kind of love that saved me: self-love.

I am about to get political, so if that isn't your thing or you might get offended, stop now...

No really...STOP!

Ok fine, but you can't say I didn't warn you...

I have to be honest; I have another ulterior motive in sharing my story at the time that I am sharing it and chose to include it as an afterthought in my book in the event that someone felt so passionately one way or the other that they could just skip it if it was that important to them. No harm. No foul. This is a very touchy subject, so I understand. Not to get political, but I'm about to get political...I am just going to say it, but I am pro-choice. I have been told that is slightly hypocritical of me, given my backstory, but I will always believe that it is up to a woman to decide what she does with her body.

Case and point. We are at a very pivotal moment in history where women's reproductive rights are being taken away, no matter the circumstances, and I find that to be incredibly wrong. I could go in on my political rant and talk about the lack of affordable housing, cost of living, the healthcare crisis, lack of maternity leave, lack of support society puts on the fathers, and the other countless reasons a woman may feel the need to terminate a pregnancy, but I won't. I want to simply come from the perspective of a child who grew up in the system. What makes me the saddest about this situation is the future victims of the broken and crooked systems that are Foster Care and the Adoption system. What will inevitably happen is that more children are going to be funneled through these systems against their will. My story was a sad one. I was one of the kids who fell through the cracks, and I barely survived; I am considered one of the lucky ones. But countless children have had it worse than me, and many don't survive. Is that fair to them? They didn't ask to be treated like an afterthought the minute they were born. Do we ever stop to think about the children that end up aging out of Foster Care? For a regular nuclear family, it is hard enough to raise children to be functioning adults. To get them through college or tech school. To set them on a life path for them to be able to thrive on their own eventually. But what about those who grow up without any support, guidance, or a sense of direction? And in most cases, of no fault of their own? A lot of foster care children grow up in one system and end up in another and get ridiculed for that as well. On the other side, adoption. There are way more families that want to adopt than there are children TO adopt, and yet, here we are. Why is that? Well one of the biggest reasons is how much it costs to adopt in America. A lot of these families could afford a child on a month-to-month basis, but the upfront costs are a different story. Where exactly does that money go? And then there is the lack of social workers.

Why do you think so many children fall through the cracks? Not enough case workers. In my opinion, social workers are the closest thing we have to saints because they don't go into this field for the big paycheck and work-life balance. They are underpaid and overworked. The horrors they must have to face...I can't even imagine. This shouldn't be a political issue. This should be an issue of basic human decency. We need to find a way to put the children first. Above profit. Above personal gain. Regulate these systems first before you try to regulate women's bodies, but I digress...

Letter to my younger self...

Dear little Lala,

Babygirl, we made it! Who would have thought? Only us, to be honest, and that is ok. I would have given anything to prevent all the horrible things that happened to you. I would have given anything to have hugged you and to have been able to tell you that everything was going to be alright, because they were. We didn't know it at the time, but they were. I would have shielded you from all the pain and suffering that you didn't deserve. I would have sat right next to you and held your hand when you were too young to fully understand what was going on. I would have yelled and screamed with you. I would have fought with you when you were hurting and didn't know why. That fire that you have within you, I wouldn't have wanted to change that for the world! And just between us girls, those boys on the playground deserved every punch to the face they got! I know you felt severely misunderstood, and that made you feel isolated and lonely. I wish I could say that feeling goes away, but it doesn't, but you do learn to make better use of that isolation in the form of your creativity. That is where you will flourish, my love! I sincerely hope that you can forgive me for when I blamed you for our circumstances. That was unfair of me. I was hurting too and needed someone to blame. I apologize for wishing that you could have been like everyone else, not knowing that what set you apart was what truly made you beautiful. You have always been and will always be a freaking force of nature! I love you, and I am so proud of you.

Your biggest fan,

Lauren

Made in the USA
Monee, IL
08 February 2025

4791ba71-4512-45fe-9010-5ba053e37da0R01